I'M JACK

Peter Kinsley was born in Northumberland and has spent his career as a journalist working in Newcastle, Manchester and Fleet Street. He was a foreign correspondent in France, Italy and Spain for various national newspapers, has written three novels, and he lives in France.

Frank Smyth was brought up in Yorkshire and at one time worked for Yorkshire local newspapers as a feature writer specializing in crime. He is now a freelance journalist and the author of several published books.

Peter Kinsley
and Frank Smyth

I'M JACK

**The Police Hunt for
the Yorkshire Ripper**

Pan Original
Pan Books London and Sydney

First published 1980 by Pan Books Ltd,
Cavaye Place, London sw10 9pg
© Peter Kinsley and Frank Smyth 1980
isbn 0 330 26111 8
Printed and bound in Great Britain by
Hazell Watson & Viney Ltd, Aylesbury, Bucks

Illustrations

Wilma McCann, aged 28. Murdered in Leeds, October 1975
Joan Harrison, aged 26. Murdered in Preston, November 1975
(*Daily Mail*, Manchester)
Emily Jackson, aged 42. Murdered in Leeds, January 1976
Irene Richardson, aged 28. Murdered in Leeds, February 1977
Patricia Atkinson, aged 33. Murdered in Bradford, April 1977
Jayne MacDonald, aged 16. Murdered in Leeds, June 1977
Jean Royle, aged 20. Murdered in Manchester, October 1977
(Press Association)
Helen Rytka, aged 18. Murdered in Huddersfield, January
1978 (Yorkshire Post Newspapers Ltd)
Yvonne Pearson, aged 22. Murdered in Bradford, January
1978 (Yorkshire Post Newspapers Ltd)
Vera Millward, aged 40. Murdered in Manchester, May 1978
(Press Association)
Josephine Whitaker, aged 19. Murdered in Halifax, April 1979
Barbara Leach, aged 20. Murdered in Bradford, September
1979 (Press Association)
The scene after Wilma McCann's body was found
(Yorkshire Post Newspapers Ltd)
A police photograph of the Yorkshire Ripper's letter sent to
George Oldfield
An intensive police search for clues (Yorkshire Post
Newspapers Ltd)
Using police dogs to cover the surrounding area for clues
(Yorkshire Post Newspapers Ltd)
George Oldfield listening to the tape of the man claiming to
be the Ripper (Press Association)
Manning the public response to hearing the Ripper tape
(Yorkshire Post Newspapers Ltd)
One of the police posters appealing for information on the
murders

Map on page 8 by Ken Smith

Name	Where found	Age	Attacked	Children
Anna Rogulski	Keighley	34	5/7/75	Divorced
Olive Smelt	Halifax	46	15/8/75	Married 3 children
Wilma McCann	Leeds	28	30/10/75	Married 4 children
Joan Harrison	Preston	26	20/11/75	2 children
Emily Jackson	Leeds	42	21/1/76	Married 3 children
Irene Richardson	Leeds	28	6/2/77	Married 2 children
Patricia Atkinson	Bradford	33	24/4/77	Married 3 children
Jayne MacDonald	Leeds	16	26/6/77	Single
Maureen Long	Bradford	42	10/7/77	3 children
Jean Royle	Manchester	20	1/10/77 (body found 10/10/77)	2 children
Marilyn Moore	Leeds	25	14/12/77	2 children
Helen Rytka	Huddersfield	18	31/1/78	Single
Yvonne Pearson	Bradford	22	21/1/78 (body found 27/3/78)	2 children
Vera Millward	Manchester	40	16/5/78	Married 7 children
Josephine Whitaker	Halifax	19	4/4/79	Single
Barbara Leach	Bradford	20	2/9/79	Single

Police in charge	Notable features
Peter Perry – head Keighley CID	*Survived*
Ronald Sills – head Halifax CID	*Survived*. Said man in his 30s
Dennis Hoban – head Leeds CID	Purse labelled MUMIY missing
Wilfred Brooks – head Preston CID	Jewellery, including wedding ring, missing
Dennis Hoban – head Leeds CID	Van driven back to original position
James Hobson – head Leeds CID	
John Domaille – head Bradford CID	Killed indoors
George Oldfield – head West Yorks CID	Worked in supermarket
George Oldfield – head West Yorks CID	*Survived*. Gave description: white; 36–37 yrs; well built; collar-length blond hair; drove white Ford Cortina with black roof
Jack Ridgeway – head Manchester CID	
George Oldfield – head West Yorks CID	*Survived*. Gave description: white; 25–28 yrs; 5 ft 6 ins; Jason King moustache and thin beard; drove maroon car
George Oldfield, assisted by John Domaille	
Trevor Lapish – head Bradford CID	
Jack Ridgeway – head Manchester CID	Setting up of 'Ripper squad' under Dick Holland
George Oldfield, assisted by Dick Holland	Worked at Halifax Building Society. No red light area
Jim Hobson, Dick Holland, assisted by Peter Gilrain – head Bradford CID	Student at Bradford University. Attacked outside red light area

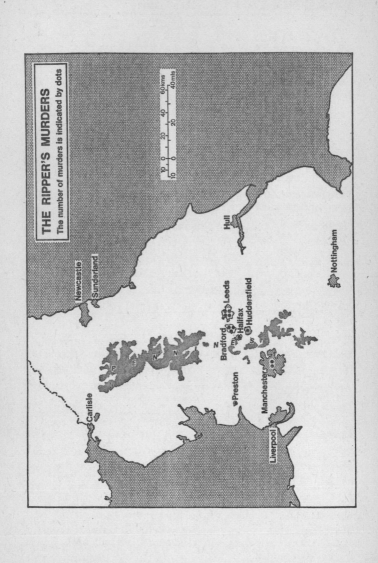

THE RIPPER'S MURDERS

The number of murders is indicated by dots

chapter one

An engineer's ball-pane hammer – sometimes known as a 'blacksmith's ball pin' – is an instrument designed to fulfil several functions in metal work. One side of the head has an ordinary, flat hammer surface, while the other, as the name suggests, is in the shape of a ball. This ball is normally used to beat out sheet metal, to hammer rivets into ships' boilers, to finish horse-shoes in a farrier's forge; its size and weight depends upon the purpose to which it is put.

On the night of Thursday, 30 October, 1975 the business end of a ball-pane hammer was cracked down on to the back of a human skull. It burst the scalp, splintered the bone and penetrated the brain, delivering a blow which stunned the victim into unconsciousness immediately.

The victim was a prostitute named Wilma McCann, and her hammer-wielding attacker a man who was to become feared throughout the north of England for the next half decade as the 'Yorkshire Ripper'.

The modern city of Leeds tries to live down its reputation for attracting prostitutes to the area known as Chapeltown. The people take pride in its history and culture, its modern buildings, its well-preserved arcades in Briggate, dating from the turn of the century. They will tell an inquirer that Leeds was mentioned in the Domesday Book as having one priest, one church and – the shape of things to come – one mill, valued at four shillings. They will talk about the high quality of the woollen cloth, the good tailoring, the money they make from light and heavy engineering, the prowess of their local football team, Leeds United, or mention their best-known native son, actor Peter O'Toole. The solid respectability of Leeds, with its three-quarter-million-odd people, its modern city centre, its smart, neat suburban houses, and gardens ablaze with flowers, its well-kept parks, cricket pitches, playing fields and recreation grounds, are the antithesis of the bad reputation it has acquired since the Chapeltown murders began in 1975.

Leeds in 1980 will be one of the world's top centres for sculpture with the new Henry Moore Gallery, containing the two million pounds worth of sculpture to be donated by Henry Moore, Yorkshire-born and trained at Leeds College of Art. The city also takes pride in its ethnic groups, who, with rare exceptions, live in close harmony with the locals.

In the same way as visitors to London from the English provinces head for Soho, looking for colour and excitement, so visitors to Leeds will visit Chapeltown by night. For there are twenty-three different nationalities in this particular district as it has traditionally been a home for immigrants ever since many of the Jews escaping from Russian pogroms early this century settled in Leeds. Then came the displaced persons from the Second World War, Jamaicans and West Indians after the war, and in recent years immigrants from Bangladesh, Pakistan, and elsewhere. Chapeltown Road, which starts amid rotting urban blight and a café selling soul food ('Salt fish and jonny cake'), has a reggae record store and a delicatessen named Riga after the capital of Latvia, a Sikh temple and a Polish club renowned for sorrel soup and cream cheese pancakes. The accents of Jamaica, Karachi and Cracow mingle with the local Yorkshire dialect, and music from wild steel bands emanates from Afro-hairdressers and shops selling frozen flying fish, yams and paw-paw.

It was in this colourful atmosphere of Chapeltown that a fierce-tempered Scotswoman, one of eleven children, previously employed as a still-room assistant at the exclusive Gleneagles Golf Club, came to settle with her four children, in 1970 – five years before she was to become the Ripper's first victim. Wilma, a 28-year-old native of Inverness, was found beaten and stabbed to death at Scott Hall Avenue, Chapeltown, Leeds, only 150 yards from her home. She had been savagely assaulted, had a fractured skull, lacerations to the scalp, and had been stabbed fifteen times in the abdomen. The body was only partly clothed although she had not been sexually assaulted, and a white plastic purse, on which her daughter Sonje had written affectionately MUMIY, was missing. It has never been found.

The night of 29 October was fine and clear when Wilma McCann set out for an evening pub crawl in Leeds. She wore white, flared trousers, a pink blouse and a short, dark blue bolero jacket. She said goodnight to her children: Sonje, aged nine, Richard, aged seven, Donna, aged six, and Angela, aged five. The eldest were to look after the youngest until Mummy returned home from work. The one thing that Wilma McCann liked most of all was her freedom – to go and do as she liked without any tiresome restrictions. She had separated from her husband Gerry, an Irish joiner from Londonderry, two years previously. She had agreed to a divorce on the grounds of her adultery, which she admitted, but had never bothered to turn up for the appointments that Gerry had fixed with a solicitor.

Gerry McCann was not too bothered about it. He had made a new life in Leeds with a girl called Pauline, and they had a daughter, Cheryl, aged two. Although he did not financially support Wilma, who boasted that she had as many as thirty men friends, he often visited the children at their school and gave them birthday presents.

Wilma McCann slipped out of the back of the house, as she always did, and went down the side of the playing field. She didn't like to let her neighbours see what time she went out of the house and what time she returned, in case they reported her for neglecting the children. 'It's none of their bloody business,' she would say to her friends and acquaintances in the city centre pubs she liked to frequent. She wore no overcoat, although the October night was going to get cold later when the pubs and clubs shut, for she also boasted that she was a hardy Scot, and a few good strong drams of whisky would keep the cold out.

As she sauntered towards the town centre, she mentally planned the pub crawl: the Regent, the Scotsman, the White Swan, the Royal Oak, perhaps the Robin Hood, and later when they shut the bars at 10.30 p.m. a bit of trolling up towards the Room at the Top club for a late night snack or curry and chips, one of her favourite meals, and she'd save money on a taxi by hitching a lift home. She had done it a hundred times before and she was an expert at persuading lorry drivers to drop her off at her house or even, as she had done before, go all the way to Scotland, on impulse, to see her parents and friends.

At the Regent pub in Kirkgate, men wearing cloth caps sat around drinking pints of beer and Guinness. On the walls were Breughel prints, and the graffiti in the lavatories followed the usual format of insular prejudice: LESS WOGS – MORE JOBS, IRA RULE and JEW PIGS. Someone had also scrawled an insult to another of the pub's clients: PLATE-FACE MCNALLY. Wilma had a couple of drinks and moved on, restless as always, in search of new people, new faces, a few laughs.

In the Scotsman, one of her favourite haunts, she found the same people, the same faces. In the lavatory the graffiti was marginally different: Instead of IRA it was ULSTER RULE OK? and VOTE NF (National Front) IF YOUR (sic) BRITISH and Oscar Wilde's quotation: WORK IS THE CURSE OF THE DRINKING CLASSES.

The evening wore on pleasantly enough and Wilma stayed for a while in the bar of the Royal Oak chatting to two friends before closing time forced her to head north to the Room at the Top club. The night was much colder when she left the city centre pubs and there was some mist about which threatened fog later. The street lights cast an orange glow and children were asking for 'Penny for the

Guy, missus,' well past their bedtime, collecting for Guy Fawkes night the following week. The delicious smell of Cantonese Chinese cooking wafted from the open doorway of the Jumbo Chinese restaurant in Vicar Lane, where the menu listed shark's fin soup, fried king prawns, scallops chow mein and Peking Capital spare ribs. Wilma, her appetite sharpened, crossed New York Road and went past the Eagle Tavern in North Street where she had often been given a lift by drivers who parked their lorries there, and on past the Golden Cross transport café, also good for lifts, and the occasional meal of gammon and eggs, towards the Room at the Top.

She stayed there until 1 a.m. when she left carrying a white plastic container with curry and chips, and then began thumbing lifts at 1.05 a.m. She was seen near Rakusen's food warehouse in Meanwood Road, by people who recognized her. A lorry driver going towards the M62 motorway to Lancaster stopped when she flagged him down, thinking she was in some sort of trouble, but when she spoke to him he declined to take her in his lorry. He last saw her at the junction of Inner Ring Road and Meanwood Road, carrying the white container, and walking towards Barrack Street and Scott Hall Road. To the left she saw the six giant fifteen-storey blocks of council flats and to the right two enormous three-storey gasometers with their rusty, flaking grey paint. In Barrack Street, on the corner behind a high wire fence, a ghostly sight at night was a group of statues of nudes, lions, flowerpots, and Hercules amongst copies of Antonio Canova's marble Venus which stands in the entrance to the Leeds art gallery.

Another lorry driver, Mr Walker, saw Wilma McCann stop a red or orange coloured fast-back car, like an Avenger, and he saw the same vehicle again at the traffic lights of Barrack Street. Wilma was sitting in the passenger seat. The driver was a coloured man, possibly West Indian, aged about 35, wearing a black donkey-jacket and a grey trilby hat. He had a full face and thin, droopy moustache. Some time shortly after getting out of this car, Wilma McCann was seen by another man – and she was just the type of person he wanted: a lone woman, out on the streets after dark.

The Ripper attacked Wilma McCann with such savagery, leaving her body in a pool of blood, that the police were to say later: 'The pattern of the stab wounds immediately brought to mind the maniacal type of homicide that sometimes occurs.' He left the body on the grassy bank of a playing field; a caretaker in a nearby bungalow twenty-five yards away, who had gone to bed at 11.30 p.m., was not awakened by the disturbance and his dog did not bark a warning. Thick fog closed in around the Prince Philip playing field as the Ripper made his escape.

At 6 a.m. eleven-year-old Tracy Attram, a neighbour of the McCann children, saw two of them waiting at a nearby bus stop in the fog. She asked them what they were doing and they said they were waiting for their mummy to come home. An hour later Mr Alan Routledge, a milkman, of Prince Edward Grove, Leeds, saw what he thought was a pile of rags. He went towards it, trying to make out the shape, when his younger brother, ten-year-old Paul, shouted: 'It's a body. It's a body.' Mr Routledge then saw it was not an old guy which had been abandoned by children, which was his second thought, but the partly clothed body of a dead woman. He ran to the caretaker's bungalow and telephoned the police.

When the police realized that it was murder, Detective Chief Superintendent Dennis A. Hoban, one of the best-liked detectives in Leeds, arrived on the scene. Mr Hoban had a reputation for obsessive tenacity and for playing 'hunches' which had helped him to solve fifty murders since he had been made inspector at the early age of thirty-three. 1975 had been a good year for Dennis Hoban. In January, three trees were planted in his honour in the Ben

Gurion cemetery in Israel and in the same month he had bravely defused a time-bomb seconds before it was due to burst into flame in Woolworths in Leeds. He was given the Queen's commendation for bravery.

The Wilma McCann murder was 'right up Dennis's street', the other policemen in Leeds said, for he had outstanding local knowledge of Chapeltown and would work forty-eight hours at a stretch on a murder inquiry.

Dennis Hoban was brought up in a tradition of duty. He liked to tell the story of his father, Patrick, who had been a Boy Scout in Scarborough, and had seen a drunken brawl between fishermen interrupted by the arrival of PC Stockdale. The fishermen had turned on the constable, knocked him into a pile of herrings, stuck him in a barrel and were about to roll him off the end of Scarborough pier when Boy Scout Hoban flung himself on the policeman, grabbed his whistle, blew the alarm, and saved him from a watery grave. He was presented with two medals for bravery and an inscribed watch by the Scarborough police.

Dennis Hoban examined Wilma McCann's body in the cold, foggy October morning. He noticed that her purse was missing and so took robbery into consideration as part of the motive. The pathologist who was brought to study the body was Professor David Gee, head of the Department of Forensic Medicine at Leeds University. This was his first look at the work of a man whose marks he was to come to know only too well. In the days that followed the body's discovery the most intensive police hunt that Leeds had known swung into operation, with 150 detectives out with questionnaires for lorry and tanker drivers, motorists and neighbours of Wilma McCann, and others setting up road-blocks for screening at Sheepscar junction.

Each morning Mr Hoban briefed the detectives to follow up and check information telephoned in by the public, and interview people for minute details of the victim's last hours, to trace and eliminate people seen in her company the last day and trace all those she met in the city's public houses that night. The vital police work, meticulous and slogging, continued day after day, and the photograph of a similar white plastic purse with the scrawled, childish writing 'MUMIY' on it was issued to the press when it was known that, apart from money, there was a photograph, which the children had seen, of a man friend of Wilma's called Tommy, whom police wanted to trace. Lorry drivers and motorists were traced and asked to make detailed statements.

The children were placed in council care until their father was contacted. Offers to adopt them and to give them a 'good home for Christmas' flooded in. Wilma's mother, Betsy Newlands said:

Wilma went to Inverness Technical School and was a good pupil, and a good speller. She was always full of life and tried to live every day in her own dynamic way. She was not a volatile girl, but she tended to get emotional very quickly – and then anybody within earshot knew about it. She liked having a good time, but it is not fair what people have said about her being a prostitute. Whatever she did she did for enjoyment. She did not deserve to go this way. Not murdered.

Wilma's sister Lilian, 34-year-old mother of two who had travelled to Leeds from London, said: 'No outsiders need offer homes to the kids. They are happy they are going to their dad, but the family would have had them.'

The police interviewed twenty-nine of Wilma McCann's men friends, but could not trace 'Tommy', the man in Wilma's life, described by the children as a slim-built, 5 ft 11 in Scot with a broad accent and black, collar-length hair with a quiff in front, whose photograph the children had seen in the purse. On 2 November they issued a photograph of a policewoman wearing McCann's clothes. On the 3rd Mr Hoban asked Wilma's children about Tommy. On Guy Fawkes day, he appealed for Tommy to come forward. The intensive search for the murder weapons, in dustbins and drains within a quarter-mile radius of Wilma's home had come to nothing. The carton containing the curry and chips was not found, nor was the white plastic purse – the purse that may well have been taken by the Ripper and kept as a souvenir of the night in Leeds that he beat and stabbed to death his first victim, Wilma McCann.

chapter two

Prostitutes in the areas where the Ripper has struck have abandoned their night beats in fear of their lives, and only a handful of 'couldn't-care-less' hardened professionals venture unaccompanied on to the streets after dark. Many operate during the afternoon hours, returning to the safety of flats, bars and hotels at dusk, which allows them several hours on the streets before lighting-up time – 9.18 p.m. in Leeds in summertime. In winter, with the sky darkening around 6 p.m., their only trade is in the bars and with regular clients. Most of the 200 prostitutes in the Leeds–Bradford area have one or two 'bread-and-butter' clients, who are often men who have visited them regularly for years and on whom they can still depend as a source of income. Many of the regular clients are Indian and Pakistani bachelors and businessmen, especially in the Bradford area and, as many of them are in the clothing trade, they usually carry large amounts of cash.

In April 1978 the Chief Constable of Yorkshire, Mr Ronald Gregory, in a meeting with six of his top detectives who are hunting the Ripper, made a tentative suggestion that prostitution should be legalized. 'It would eliminate a lot of these vicious attacks,' he said, 'but I do not think a lot of prostitutes would want it – they prefer private enterprise. Some of them are operating in twos, but some could not care less.'

His remarks led to the usual outraged replies from churchmen. The Bishop of Wakefield, the Right Rev. Colin James said:

Christians would find this repugnant. The danger is that if you legalized prostitution people would look on it as all right to indulge in. Sex outside marriage debases the whole idea of relations between two people.

The Provost of Bradford, the Very Rev. Brandon Jackson, said:

To put this immoral trade above the counter rather than underneath it would indeed be to give greater safety to these poor, wretched women. But the price we would pay for that would be an altogether lower standard of behaviour and would undermine the principle of morality in our society.

After each vicious murder, police have patrolled streets and warned prostitutes to stay off the streets after dark, or work in pairs, taking car numbers when their companion goes with a client. Heeding this warning, and afraid to go with clients in cars after the Ripper murders in Bradford, four prostitutes there started to do business in a house in Belle Vue, Manningham, in February 1978. The police raided the house after a few days and the women were charged with keeping a brothel. The prosecuting solicitor said that from the observations of the vice squad it appeared the prostitutes were loath to go into cars. A 26-year-old prostitute admitted keeping the brothel, another aged 36 was given a three months prison sentence suspended for two years, and two others, a 26 year old and a 17 year old, were each put on probation for two years for assisting in the management of a brothel.

In Leeds, as far back as 1975, the coloured community of Chapeltown, increasingly concerned about the stigma being placed on coloured women in the area, issued a thousand leaflets entitled *Chapeltown Acts Against Prostitution,* and posed the question: 'How many times has your teenage daughter on her way home from school been accosted by men in cars asking her what her price is?

In the four years that have passed since that leaflet was distributed, the attitudes of the Chapeltown prostitutes have changed completely. When BBC Radio Leeds took their microphones on to the streets after the last Chapeltown murder and asked for opinions, one replied:

I'm terrified by him, afternoon or night. Summat to do with a doctor, I reckon he is. Because he does a neat job cutting them. I may have my throat cut. It's just a chance you take. It's hard to find work so I do this. You need the money. Yes, I'm ashamed of the situation I've got myself into. The Ripper's very fly.

Another said:

I'm scared to go out by myself. I'm scared to go out even if it's light. I don't go to any lonely places without somebody with me. We all knew the girl [Jayne MacDonald, who lived in the area]. She was a right nice girl. It's terrible that someone of sixteen should be killed. I'm going home now – early. My parents have said 'Get in early'. There are three of us operating together. We don't want to get involved, really. We don't want our names in the paper or on the radio.

Detective Chief Superintendent Jim Hobson told the BBC: 'This year we have arrested or cautioned seventy prostitutes. There is still a hard core in existence here. No, there will be no amnesty for them. We have taken steps to stamp out prostitution, although I know it's the oldest profession in the world.'

At the height of the publicity about the Ripper murders in Chapeltown, Leeds, a 'teeny-bopper' prostitute aged 17 pleaded guilty to soliciting. Her friend, also 17, pleaded not guilty to loitering for prostitution. They had asked police officers in an unmarked patrol car: 'Were you looking for business? It's five pounds.' The first was given a conditional discharge and the second had the charge dismissed. The police officers were told by the first teenager: 'I need the money because I can't get work.'

On 15 June, 1979 the local evening newspaper headlined a story: 'Good Time Girls Flee Shadow of the Ripper' and revealed how prostitutes from Chapeltown had been driven on to the Continent out of fear. In an interview, one girl, Patricia Manning, who has two children, aged six and four, living in Leeds whom she visits every month, said: 'Since he struck, lots of girls have left the streets.' Since January 1979 she had been working as a dancer in a Zurich night club along with several other Yorkshire girls who left because of fear of the Ripper. She now saves £700 a month out of the £1,000 she is paid, by living off the commission she earns getting customers to order expensive champagne.

Leaving the children for a month at a time doesn't seem too bad. I once spent three months inside when I was hustling. Since the Ripper struck a lot of girls work in pubs or in pairs and a lot more have gone to London. I come from the north east, like the Ripper is supposed to. I came down to stay with a relative in Leeds for a week. I got involved with a fella, fell pregnant and couldn't go home because my parents were funny about that sort of thing. I was seventeen then. So I went on the game. I feel much better doing this dancing job now. Before, if I had £30 I'd just go out and blow it without thinking. The £1,000 a month I get now is no more than I earned on the streets charging 'punters' £10 a time. Most of the girls had kids like I did, with no fella to back them up. I used to get £18 a week from the Social Security. Take £10 rent from that and you don't have much left to look after yourself and two kids. You just have to get money and hustling is the easiest, quickest way of doing it. I'll work in Zurich for another three or four months to get the house furnished properly. After that I don't know what I'll be doing.

In February 1979 the editor of the *Halifax Courier* sent out girl reporter Diane Crabtree to talk to some of the Leeds prostitutes all of whom gave fictitious names. One attractive brunette, 'Sara', talked about the time she let a client have sex on credit.

He had a knife at my throat. I panicked like mad and told him he could have credit. I'd been with him two or three times before, in Chapeltown, and he'd been straight, so I didn't hesitate when he pulled up. I remember him leaning forward into the glove compartment to get what I thought was his money. The next thing I knew he had a big knife at my throat. He was desperate for sex but he didn't have any money. So I told him he could pay me later . . .

Sara told the reporter how Chapeltown had changed during the past few years since the Ripper murders, and how she was finding it difficult to make a living. She confessed that she had no great love for the police and said the girls relied on help from each other rather than from them. 'If the Ripper struck again they wouldn't care, it would be just one more off their territory.' But a police officer who was questioned the same day said: 'To say we don't care is neither fair nor true. In fact, we are probably the only ones who do care.'

She said that six years ago she was in her heyday, but admitted that, at 27 years of age, her 'days are numbered'. 'It's all the Ripper's fault, you know,' she said. 'In the old days Chapeltown used to be a fantastic place for prostitutes. There was always plenty of work. Now the men daren't come. The younger, prettier girls still come, though. And, because they are new, they take away the few punters that there are. You can always tell an out-of-town girl. She'll wiggle her bottom and think she's God's gift to men and she'll get away with soliciting because the police don't know her.'

'Many of the girls in Chapeltown work for pimps,' said Sara, who has twenty-seven convictions for prostitution. 'One friend of mine used to earn about £100 a week and had to hand over every penny to the man she worked for and lived with. He used to give her £5 back, to buy tights and contraceptives.'

The girl known as the queen of Bradford prostitutes, petite 22-year-old 'Skip', who has been 'on the game' since she was 15 when she ran away from home, said:

If I thought about the Ripper every time I was on the street, I'd run home and lock the door. I stop myself thinking about him by thinking about *money*. It always works. Prostitution should be legalized. If there were not prostitutes there would be more rape and therefore a lot more work for the police. We are carrying out a service and not hurting anyone. A lot of girls I know would be unemployed and living off the state. The public should look up to us instead of looking down their noses at us. I look down at people who are on the dole – those that can get work but won't – and I feel I'm ten times better than they are. At least I'm earning a living.

Skip's most tolerated client is a minor tycoon who is happily married to a woman who doesn't think sex is necessary to the over 40s. 'He pays for his cars, clothes and meals – it's simpler and more sensible to pay for his sex too, I suppose. He is generous too. He once gave me £100 to pay off a fine so I didn't have to go to prison. But they're not all charitable. I always take money off punters in advance. Some have the cheek to ask for it back afterwards. You've got to be straight and tough with them. I keep a chopper under my bed.'

Skip despises the idea that prostitutes are dirty, untidy, and 'not nice to know'. 'Bath oils and cleaners are what I spend my money on – I take a bath as often as I can. I also visit the VD clinic regularly for a check-up. I have a responsibility to my regular clients. And it may surprise you to know,' she told the reporter, 'that I've got a swear box next to my bed. I don't swear. It's for visitors.'

Another girl, aged 19, who has been 'on the game' since she was 15, dark-eyed and beautiful 'Sasha' of Huddersfield, with a model's figure and dusky skin, confessed that she had a chip on her shoulder as a result of being a prostitute. She had an arrogant, brash, couldn't-care-less attitude towards the Ripper. 'If I get him, I get him, and that's all there is to it. I don't really care. No one would miss me, only my young son Justin, who is the only one I work and care for.' The tough exterior was probably a front for her insecurity, for she had turned to drink to give herself confidence and had started looking for business in the afternoons, taking her street or regular clients back to the one-bedroomed flat which she shares with another prostitute.

She confessed that the Ripper was not the worrying thing on her mind. 'I'm afraid of him, but I'm more afraid of going into prison. I couldn't stand it.' Most of Sasha's customers are married men, whom she charges £10. 'Is that for half an hour?' Diane asked her. There was a burst of laughter. 'That's for ten minutes – at the most,' she said. On a good afternoon, she earns £50, 'but no matter what I earn, I always need more. I've tried saving but it's impossible. I suppose I spend what I have because I know at the back of my mind there's always more where it came from.'

Sasha would not talk about her son's father or her own parents, and she said that she hates sex and hates men even more. 'A lot of men think only about their own satisfaction. They are like animals,' she said.

Many of the plainclothes policemen and uniformed men on the Ripper hunt are on first-name terms with the prostitutes of Leeds, Huddersfield and Bradford, as their beat covers the pub-club circuit where the girls operate. One of the Ripper Squad men said:

We treat them with respect and get the same in return. But it wasn't always like that. We have had to convince them we are their friends, not their enemies. Most of them are suspicious of anybody. It's the pimps – the men they work for – who hate our presence. The girls daren't talk to us when they are about, and we have great difficulty in nailing any of them because the girls are too frightened to give evidence against them.

The detective had just returned from a prostitute's home where he had warned the woman's son about stealing from his mother's purse. 'She asked me to speak to him as a favour, and I did because it's all part of the job.'

When we began our research in Bradford in the summer of 1979, we found that it was 'business as usual' in the haunts of prostitutes – even in the bars which had been frequented by three of the murdered women: Patricia Atkinson, Yvonne Pearson and Helen Rytka. They had come off the streets after dark, but dozens of them, professional prostitutes and good time girls who would do a 'trick' if they met what they thought was the right type of client, crowded the music bars and disco-rooms of the Queens, the Flying Dutchman and the Perseverance, despite all the publicity and the police warnings about the danger they were in.

The girls drank soft drinks, Pils lager or Special Brew until they picked up a client and then switched to hard liquor: large gin and tonic, large brandy and port, large whisky. They all had nicknames: Black Bess, Liverpool Alice, Brown Ale Mary. One called simply Sally said:

We used to have the area to ourselves, but now most of the operators round here come in from outside: from Wakefield, Leeds and Liverpool, and some from as far away as Glasgow, Nottingham and even London, when it's too 'hot' for them there. Some of us have spells down south, too, for the same reason, or to hit the Arab trade. Yvonne Pearson and her mate used to go down and 'do' the south once or twice a year, a sort of 'holiday' you might say, especially if they could roll an Ay-rab. But here, the Paki bachelors are the big draw. They're mostly in business with quite a few quid which they carry around with them in cash. Of course they don't get much in the way of sex from their own girls – too strict, you know – so they come to us.

The men are often in as much danger from the girls as the prostitutes are from the odd sadistic client. The whores of Lumb Lane in Bradford, once called the most vicious street in Europe by a British Sunday newspaper, take pride in their toughness and their ability to 'roll' a client. 'One girl I know,' said Sally, 'picked up a young Indian in a boozer and took him back to her pad. While he was on the job her mate came out of hiding and whacked him unconscious. They robbed him of all his bread and off they went down south for a while.'

A tall girl named Dotty, a red-head of 38, who cheerfully admitted to having been 'on the game' since she was 15, expressed her love and loyalty to the coloured community of Bradford's Manningham area: 'I particularly like the West Indians,' she said. 'They're a cheerful lot. They always make me laugh. If I like one in particular I'll do a "trick" for him for nowt if trade is slack. But not all my customers are nice,' she added, opening her handbag and producing a pair of long-bladed hairdresser's scissors. She went on:

A lot of girls have been carrying something like this since the killings started. There was an approach to the police to get us permission to carry tear gas or Mace or whatever it's called, to fight off an attacker, but it was a definite no to that. This is England, after all, and an offensive weapon is an offensive weapon. Besides, I think they thought we might blast the odd client and roll him if we had tear gas. One copper said why didn't we carry sticks? Sticks? I ask you. I mean, who's going to pick a girl up if she's carryin' a fuckin' big stick?

The prostitutes of Lumb Lane, although tolerating girls from outside the area, do not like them coming in from Manchester. 'They have their own beat in Moss Side, and their own scene,' one girl said. 'Besides which, they are hard bitches in Lancashire. They take a client back for a short time and then say: "It'll cost you an extra three pounds if I take me bra off." Hard as bloody nails they are over there.' They still talk of the ingenious stroke pulled by one prostitute in Lumb Lane, who secreted her small son in a false-fronted chest of drawers, which was in fact a small cupboard. While the Indian businessman client was totally distracted, the boy came silently out of the chest of drawers, stole the bulging wallet from the man's jacket on the back of a chair, crept silently back and made an exit through a hole in the wall to disappear with the money. The Indian called the police, who asked if he had seen the woman take his money. 'No. She didn't take it,' he said. 'I just cannot understand it. There was definitely nobody else in the room at the time.'

The proprietor of one haunt of Bradford prostitutes said:

I feel sorry for these girls. They take a terrible risk. Many of their clients are frustrated immigrant men who cannot have sex with their own women outside marriage because of moral or religious hang-ups. But other clients are bloody sadists. The girls come in here with black eyes, bruises all over their bodies and with burn marks on the forearms and thighs. Some of their clients pay them just so that they can burn them with cigarette ends or punch them up – getting their own back on women, I suppose. Like the rotten bastard who calls himself the Ripper.

In September 1976 when the Ripper murders frightened girls out of Leeds and Bradford, people in the Forest Road area of Nottingham complained to the police that a mini-bus was being used to drop young prostitutes from Leeds and Derby in Hyson Green, their red light area. The girls, some of them only sixteen, thought it safer there, and were

accosting schoolboys on their way home. Later the prostitute population of Hyson Green doubled because of the
Ripper scare, and each girl would have a lengthy chat with
a client before entering his car, and if she did get driven
away one of her friends took the car number and destroyed
it in front of the client when he returned her.

In March 1979 the joint central committee of the
Police Federation – Britain's police 'union' – recommended
that prison sentences for convicted prostitutes should be
scrapped. The Commons Expenditure Committee, investigating women and the penal system, was given this recom-
mendation on the grounds that the majority of women
prostitutes are inadequate, suffering from drug addiction,
alcoholism or have suicidal tendencies or a history of mental
disorders.

Prostitutes interviewed in the Leeds, Bradford and
Manchester areas echoed this view and confirmed that one
of the problems for social workers with young prostitutes
is that if they run away from home, go 'on the game' and
get caught, they are put into local care. They then abscond
and while on the run, return to prostitution to support
themselves, whereas a boy on the run would steal and get
caught. One girl said:

Once you get into this way of life you cannot give it up. I
never think about what I am doing or what is happening. But
no man ever goes away dissatisfied. If it is straight sex I expect
to spend about three minutes with them – not counting
undressing and dressing. I charge £8 or £10. If any deviation
is required the charge trebles or quadruples. If ever I got
interested in a client or excited by him, I'd have to stop
hustling. There is a need for prostitution, or the otherwise
happily married man who comes to me for what his wife isn't
prepared to give him would not pay my wages. As long as I
can get £8 for three minutes, why give up? They're right about
prison, though. I never met a pro. yet who had been cured by
a spell inside.

An 18-year-old prostitute in Manchester also got £8 or £10 on the streets, but said she stopped work when she had made £30. 'I never let them feel me up or kiss me. I never look at their faces and I don't feel anything,' she said.

In Leeds, Bradford, Huddersfield and Manchester, the prostitutes interviewed fell into different categories, just as people in any other profession fall into categories, but it would be a mistake to generalize about any of them. There are the tough, elderly, sad women, often with two or three or more children to support, who could not live on Social Security, and will go with lorry drivers or drunks for five pounds; then there are the hardened professionals who like the life and find prostitution the easiest and quickest way of getting quite large sums of money; some save, some squander, but for all, their lives as prostitutes are as limited by years as those of ballet dancers or top sportsmen. There are 'hard' cases who hate men, and 'soft' touches who like men too much, and yet others who are simply doing the best they can for their children. During the past five years they have all risked being murdered in the most horrific way at the hands of the Ripper, and yet they can all still talk cheerfully about their lives.

'The trouble with writing – or talking, even – about the Ripper,' said 'Jenny', a 28-year-old Yorkshire newspaper reporter, 'is that the man is mad enough to do anything. This is why most prostitutes won't give you their correct names in an interview, and I admit that it is the reason I have asked my news editor not to by-line my copy when I write about these killings. All right, so far he has only killed lone women, at night, in secluded places. But who can fathom the mind of a person like this? If I have my name published in a book or even in the newspaper I work for in connection with his activities, what is to stop him coming round to the office and asking for me and then belting me one? Or even worse, following me from work and attacking me?'

Therefore 'Jenny' is not the speaker's real name. Despite these words, however, she is neither hysterical nor naïve. A Cambridge graduate, she has been a newspaper reporter since leaving university and has written on most aspects of crime and sociological problems: wife beating, prostitution and rape, as well as covering several murders in depth. But like many intelligent northern women, the Ripper has brought out a streak of caution in her which, she says, she never realized existed.

The Ripper is such an unknown quantity that when writing about him one never knows whether or not one is giving him ideas. I am convinced that he relishes publicity, but that his need for it will eventually bring about his downfall. On the other hand, what would bring him more publicity than the murder of a newspaper reporter who had written about him, or a policewoman engaged in the hunt for him? This may all sound very silly but I don't give a damn. I can't begin to understand the convolutions of the man's mind – so I am being extremely cautious until he is caught.

Another girl reporter said:

It came home to me with a terrible thud when I was sent to cover the Josephine Whitaker murder. We could all see her lying there on the playing field, her face peeping from under the screen the police had covered her with, and I kept thinking: 'My God, this could be me or my sister or my mother. This is an ordinary working girl, and this is *not* a red light area.' Jayne MacDonald *could* have been mistaken for a pro. walking home through Chapeltown at almost three o'clock in the morning, but I know there are no professional whores in Halifax – a few enthusiastic amateurs in the city centre bars, perhaps, but which town in the world doesn't have that? It's not so long ago we read about people waiting at parties in New York until all had got a taxi to take them home because of 'muggings' and we used to think it couldn't happen here – well, it does. No girl with any sense will walk home from a party after dark in any of these towns where there has been a murder.

She is by no means alone among normally self-confident women journalists in the north – who only a few years ago were insisting on their right to equal opportunity in covering potentially dangerous jobs such as political demonstrations and bomb scares. With the Ripper scare, the situation has changed and if a tip-off reaches a newspaper office late, or the information about an incident is incorrect, they can easily find themselves in a deserted district, alone and vulnerable.

One Manchester reporter in her 20s described how her imagination flared when her night editor rushed her out to a suburban estate. The newspaper had been told that a fleet of fire engines and ambulances was racing towards the scene of a serious gas explosion. She swiftly discovered that the emergency had been exaggerated; the firemen were pulling away from the address mentioned in the 999 message. It was either a hoax alarm or what the emergency services term a 'false alarm with good intent'. The girl, well-trained and competent, knew that her next move was to inform her office that there was no story. Edition time was approaching and her immediate need was to telephone. She recalled:

I drove round the quiet streets and many of the street lights were out of action because of damage. I suddenly felt very apprehensive. When I parked near a telephone kiosk, I felt vulnerable as I opened the car door. It was only about fifteen yards across a grass verge, but I didn't hang about. I ran, threw open the door, and dived in – only to discover that the handset had been vandalized. Outside there were distant patches of light shining through drawn curtains. The only sounds as I fled back to the car were the kiosk door closing behind me, the wind around the chimney pots, and the sound of my comfortable driving shoes slapping the grass. Perhaps it was irrational, I don't know. But I put my foot down and broke every rule of good driving until I reached the well-lit, busy main road and a telephone which was still working. Today, I am still prepared to do my stint of night duties, but that one incident made me much more careful.

Four of the Ripper's victims were struck down in the neighbourhood of hospitals – the Wythenshawe Hospital, Manchester, St James's Hospital, Leeds, the Halifax Royal Infirmary and the Manchester Royal Infirmary. This, of course, may well be coincidence, but the fact is not lost on nurses who work round the clock and frequently leave the wards when towns and cities are closing down for the night. A Bradford nursing sister, a well-balanced, mature woman in her 30s, admitted: 'If I have to travel by myself after dark, I always make sure my collapsible umbrella is handy and I always look around carefully before I get out of my car. Maybe I am over-reacting. After all, the Ripper has never gone for a nurse or anyone else in uniform for that matter.'

Since the dark advent of the Ripper, barmaids, night club staff, bus conductresses, supermarket assistants – even wives considering an evening cookery or car-maintenance class in a school or college surrounded by playing fields – think twice before making a solitary walk. West Yorkshire police have emphasized repeatedly that any woman within striking distance could become the next victim: it is not only in 'red light areas' that risks are present. A park, or any lonely road could provide the backcloth for murder, which is why wise women and their husbands, fathers and boyfriends have been advised to change their lifestyle and be on guard.

One Leeds businessman, father of two daughters aged 15 and 17, outlined the sensible attitude:

The Ripper has struck against perfectly ordinary lasses already. I think our daughters appreciate the dangers warned of by police, but we are making sure for our own peace of mind. Even if the girls do think of me as an old kill-joy, there is no way they are going to be allowed to find their own way home. If they go to a dance or a party I collect them in the car. After all, Chapeltown is only ten minutes away from many residential areas of Leeds. If they get regular, steady boyfriends we know and can trust I might leave the responsibility to them – until then I pick them up.

chapter three

Detective Superintendent Dick Holland is a big, burly man with Mephistophelean eyebrows and a reputation for being one of the best detectives in Britain. He is taciturn, tenacious, and brooks nonsense from absolutely no one – all qualities traditionally shared by the finest Yorkshiremen and the finest policemen.

Since mid-1978, Dick Holland has been in charge of an élite core of men hunting the Yorkshire Ripper. Officially they have no collective name, although official press releases usually refer to them as the 'Ripper Squad'. To begin with the team was twelve detectives strong, which naturally earned them the nickname 'The Dirty Dozen'. Later, as more men were draughted some wag at Millgarth Police Headquarters in Leeds dubbed them the 'Special Homicide Investigation Team', and if the acronym is cynical, it is at least apt.

'It's very hard not to get cynical, dealing with murders such as these over a protracted length of time,' said one police officer. 'Cynicism and a touch of humour help to keep us objective in our inquiries. Without them even experienced detectives would risk breakdowns, dealing with the brutality and heartbreak this man has doled out.'

It was not the police team's self-inflicted nickname which provoked accusations of 'flippancy' among certain hostile sections of the press, however, but a wry, off the cuff remark delivered at a press conference by Dick Holland.

'Are you going to call in Scotland Yard?' asked one reporter.

'Why should we?' came the immediate reply. 'They haven't caught their own Ripper yet.'

In fact, as Mr Holland explained, 'calling in the Yard' is no longer the semi-automatic procedure that it was in the past, when small local police forces often lacked the facilities to deal efficiently with a murder inquiry, and when the New Scotland Yard buildings on the Thames embankment housed the only really sophisticated crime fighting outfit – complete with fingerprints, ballistics, and scientific departments – in Britain. In those days, too, 'calling in the Yard' often revolved around the matter of money.

Each provincial county, city, or borough force had its own watch committee which, among other things, regulated police expenditure. If Scotland Yard's assistance was requested within twenty-four hours of a murder being discovered, the expense devolved upon them, and not the local rates. A longer delay meant that the locals bore the brunt.

Newspapers in those days usually reported that 'Scotland Yard's Murder Squad' had appeared at the scene of the local crime. In practice, the average appeal for Yard help produced two officers – usually a detective superintendent and a detective constable, though more senior officers often attended a serious or difficult crime, and they worked under the local head of crime to see that the proper investigative procedures were carried out. The Yard's 'murder squad' was, and is, a flexible unit which changes form and size according to circumstances and draws its personnel from detectives with experience of homicide. Its most famous asset, the so-called 'murder bag' was in fact the invention of a Home Office pathologist, the late Sir Bernard Spilsbury.

In 1924, Spilsbury was called to the south coast of England to investigate a crime in which a man named Mahon had killed and dismembered his girl-friend Emily Kaye, boiling some of the pieces in an effort to destroy them. When Spilsbury arrived he saw to his horror that a police superintendent was handling the dreadful remains with his bare hands. Making inquiries, he discovered that the police had no special equipment for use at the scene of a murder. As a result, Spilsbury and Dr Scott Gillett introduced the 'murder bag' which is kept packed and ready to be taken on an inquiry. It contains such items as rubber gloves, a hand lens, a tape measure, a straight-edge ruler, swabs, sample bags, forceps, scissors, a scalpel and other instruments which might be called for.

Again, the 'murder bag' was quickly adopted by provincial forces and was not the exclusive prerogative of Scotland Yard.

At one time the presence of a London-based Home Office pathologist such as Sir Bernard Spilsbury could make a great difference to a local murder inquiry. In the case of Yorkshire police forces, however, this has not been so for many years; the department of forensic medicine at Leeds University, currently headed by Professor David Gee, has long been regarded as one of the best in Europe.

Some West Yorkshire police officers with long memories take an understandable delight in quoting at least one case in which Yard men were left with egg on their faces. Before the reorganization of regional forces in 1968, the Dewsbury Borough Police were a separate unit from the West Riding Constabulary, whose territory surrounded them. One night an old prostitute was found dead in a doorway, her scalp split open and her knickers around her ankles. It looked like murder, and the watch committee hastily decided to save money and call in Scotland Yard.

Two London officers duly arrived, examined the body and the scene of the crime, patronized local detectives and ordered suit lengths from local mills, which produced excellent woollen cloth. Several days passed with no positive result, until a few days later another body was discovered in identical circumstances, but this time in Batley Carr, a few hundred yards outside Dewsbury Borough's jurisdiction, in West Yorkshire territory. A detective sergeant from the local station and a Batley police doctor had 'solved the crime' within half an hour. A few brief inquiries and an investigation of the ground showed that the second woman had been in the habit of soliciting in the area. She had gone around the corner to urinate and while crouched down had suffered a heart attack; unable to pull up her knickers, she had nevertheless staggered a few yards into a shop doorway and had fallen over, cracking her head before she died.

A cursory examination of the facts of the first death in Dewsbury showed that by sheer coincidence, a similar sequence of events had occurred there. The Yard men took the first train home.

It was this sort of incident which finally revealed the anomaly of having dozens of small forces, not only in Yorkshire but in the whole of the British Isles, and in part led to the regional reorganization of the police, in 1974.

The hierarchy of the West Yorkshire Metropolitan Police, as the new force became known, appears complex at first glance, but is in fact streamlined in its simplicity. At the head of the force is the chief constable, Mr Ronald Gregory, assisted by a deputy chief constable, Mr Austin Hayward. Immediately answerable to the chief constable's office are six assistant chief constables, each with their area of responsibility, and equivalent in rank to Scotland Yard's commanders; they head crime, road traffic, organization, personnel and training, and the 'western' and 'eastern' areas into which the force is split.

The western and eastern areas each consist of seven divisions, whose boundaries are shaped according to such factors as population and acreage. Into the western area fall the towns of Huddersfield, Halifax, and Bradford, while Leeds and Wakefield occupy the eastern area. Huddersfield and Halifax Divisions are themselves split into three sub-divisions; the rest are sub-divided into two. Heading each division is a chief superintendent and a superintendent, while each sub-division is also headed by a superintendent. Under the sub-divisional superintendent comes a chief inspector, and below him five inspectors and one detective inspector, in charge of the sub-divisional Criminal Investigation Department.

It is at this point that apparent complications ensue, in the form of the actual running of the CID as a whole. Immediately answerable to the assistant chief constable (crime), are three detective chief superintendents, each with a superintendent immediately below them, and these three are technically in charge of the CID in the western and eastern areas and of the Wakefield CID headquarters, which, in criminal matters only, forms a third area – the southern. Every division has a detective chief inspector in charge of its CID who is in the potentially embarrassing position of being equally answerable not only to his divisional chief superintendent but also to his area detective chief superintendent. In fact, common sense prevents any head-on clashes; but, as an officer explained: 'If there were a difference of opinion the divisional chief would probably have the final word on most things.'

In addition to run-of-the-mill investigation work, the CID can call upon several specialist squads and sections: the Burglary Squad, Fraud Squad, Drugs Squad, Serious Crimes Squad – which does not specifically include murder, but is often involved in the examination of unlawful killings – the small but busy Obscene Publications Squad, and the Mounted, Dogs, and Underwater Search Sections, as well as Firearms and Special Branches.

Despite these diverse activities going on within the one force, 1977 saw the Home Office dabbling with regional organization once again, and large, obdurate senior police boots were put gently but firmly down on too much Whitehall interference. One of the results was the formation of the Area Task Forces.

These units consist of approximately fifty to sixty men, about one third of them detectives, who are 'loaned' to any division for special jobs which might prove a drain on local manpower. They come under the command of the area detective chief superintendent, and deal with anything from a rash of burglaries to football crowd control, from National Front marches and hooliganism to door to door inquiries on a large scale – such as those concerning the Ripper hunt. Task Force officers undergo regular physical training sessions, firearm training, and regular refresher courses in investigative work and community relations.

'We are not in any way related to the Metropolitan Police's "Special Patrol Groups",' said a spokesman for the Task Force. 'We handle everything as delicately and with as little fuss as we can. We are not élitist – there is no "firearms élite" among us, for instance, although most of us can handle handguns, rifles, and so forth very efficiently if called upon to do so. The main drawback is that we are often called upon to work long and arduous periods of duty.'

It was largely from the three Area Task Forces that, in April 1978, Detective Chief Superintendent John Domaille drew the nucleus of what was to become the 'Ripper Squad'. By that time the Ripper had killed nine women, seven of them in Yorkshire, and the facts were that, though men from the divisions and sub-divisions in which the crimes had been committed were familiar with every detail of their own 'Ripper job', no one knew everything about all of them.

The remedy was a separate corps of detectives, at first led by Mr Domaille – who later was placed in charge of the West Yorkshire Metropolitan Police Academy at Wakefield – and subsequently by Dick Holland. Towards the latter half of 1979, 259 officers, including 120 detectives, were working full time with Ripper Squad men; each one is a specialist, with every known fact about his quarry at his fingertips.

To back them up, the Ripper Squad have the scene-of-crime and fingerprint sections of force headquarters under their head, Detective Chief Inspector Peter Swann. To investigate all the team's findings, the north eastern forensic science laboratory at Wetherby under its director Peter Cobb remains open twenty-four hours a day; Wetherby incorporates all the latest scientific crime-fighting aids and, costing over £1.5 million in the late 1970s, is rated as one of the finest establishments of its kind in the world.

As a police spokesman said: 'We have the men, with local knowledge and top training. We have the scientific aids and we have been on the Ripper case since it started. All a Yard man could do would be read our files and confirm our findings. Believe me, if we thought it would help, we'd call them in. But it wouldn't.'

Perhaps the most famous man of the whole investigation is Godfrey A. Oldfield, otherwise known as George. As assistant chief constable (crime) he has been in overall charge of the Ripper case since it forced him away from what should have been a purely administrative desk. A ruddy faced, bespectacled man, who looks more like a country farmer than a policeman, and who closely resembles 'M' in the James Bond films, George Oldfield has become more obsessed than any of his men with the nature and motives of his quarry.

Essentially, Mr Oldfield is a private man, living in a suburban house outside Huddersfield with his wife and three children. Some of his colleagues claim that the Ripper's crimes have added an extra edge to his perception as a detective. His first daughter would have been in her early twenties – a similar age to some of the killer's victims – had she lived. In fact she died of leukaemia when she was six. George Oldfield does not know whether her tragedy affected his job. 'There are so many tragic ways to die without being murdered,' he once said. 'The whole thing certainly made me more mature. As a detective you often see and understand the agony and grief and misery the loss of life, particularly a young life, causes. It has never been difficult for me to feel for these people.'

George Oldfield was born in 1924 at Monk Fryston, a Yorkshire country village, and after attending Archbishop Holgate School, York, he joined the navy and served on minesweepers, took part in the D Day landings, and was demobbed as a petty officer in 1946. He joined the police force then and apart from a few years in uniform he has been a detective ever since.

Of the tape recording sent to him by the man who calls himself Jack the Ripper, he said: 'I don't regard it as taunting or boastful. The voice is almost sad, a man fed up with what he has done, fed up with himself. A man who feels he knows me enough almost to take me into his confidence.'

chapter four

On 20 November, 1975, exactly one week after the police in Leeds issued the description of the coloured man in the Avenger car in which Wilma McCann had last been seen alive, Mrs Joan Harrison, 26-year-old prostitute and mother of two, who also called herself by the name of Collinson, left a friend's house at 10.25 p.m. She was wearing a considerable amount of jewellery and her handbag contained a diary listing appointments. Her disappearance was not reported in the area of Avenham, Preston, Lancashire, where she lived, but it is ironic that while the massive hunt was taking place for the Ripper in Leeds, he had struck again in Preston, more than sixty miles away, and for the second time there were items missing when the body was found, so that police believed the motive was robbery.

A woman passing the open door of a derelict garage in Berwick Street on 23 November, three days after Mrs Harrison was last seen alive, saw the crumpled figure in the gloom. The police and pathologist who examined the body saw that it had the same horrific head wounds, but at that time there was no exchange of information between the police forces of Leeds, Yorkshire and Preston, Lancashire. From the disused garage where she had been found murdered, police moved on to question hundreds of people in Preston and in the public houses frequented by Joan Harrison. The insignificant items appearing in local newspapers suggested the motive was robbery, because the body had been stripped of all jewellery and not sexually assaulted.

Detective Superintendent Wilfred Brooks told a press conference that the diary would hold a vital clue, and two days later asked pawnbrokers and dealers in Manchester to watch out for listed items of jewellery. 'If we can recover it, it would be an invaluable breakthrough in the hunt for this savage killer,' he said.

The inquest on Joan Harrison was opened and adjourned on 25 November, and the coroner said that she was the victim of a 'brutal assault'.

It was to be two years before Detective Chief Superintendent John Domaille, one of the men leading the Ripper hunt and head of Bradford CID, announced that there were similarities between the Leeds killings and the Preston murder, that his twelve-man Ripper team had reopened the file on the unsolved Preston killing, and that they intended to interview prostitutes individually throughout April and May of 1978.

Joan Harrison's jewellery, including her gold wedding ring, and Wilma McCann's plastic purse, were now believed to have been taken by the same man – the Ripper.

In January 1976, ten weeks after the murder of Wilma McCann in Chapeltown, another prostitute in Burley, Leeds, and her three-year-old son, Alan, were murdered in their home in Greenhow Crescent. Police linked the deaths of the women – both blondes – and said a similar type of murder weapon had been used.

Barbara Booth, aged 24, had fifteen stab wounds on her body. She had last been seen alive at 3.20 p.m. on Wednesday, 7 January, standing on the doorstep of her home. Mr Hoban said both women were prostitutes and appealed to other prostitutes to help catch their killer. 'Any street girls, models on the seamier side of Leeds, and the prostitutes who may know or suspect a particular client that may be this way inclined – and violently opposed to their way of life – should come forward.' He promised secrecy to Mrs Booth's clients if they would come forward. A list of clients found at her home was extensive and listed men as far away as Darlington.

Mrs Booth ran a part-time business as a 'model', posing

for photographs in bizarre clothing and in obscene positions. She advertised as a prostitute in shop windows and 'contact' magazines. She had frequented the same clubs and had the same acquaintances as Mrs McCann.

A man between 45 and 50, 5 ft 6 ins tall, with short grey hair was seen leaving the house at 3.40 p.m. on that fateful day.

Two other murders were also linked with the Ripper killings: that of Mrs Renee McGowan, aged 55, strangled in her flat in Evans Towers, Bradford, and of schoolgirl Lesley Moleseed of Rochdale, who was stabbed and buried in moorland, near Ripponden. Later, police eliminated all three – Booth, McGowan and Moleseed – from the Ripper hunt after forensic evidence and reports discounted the link.

It was not until the summer of 1977 that the police, looking for more clues on the Ripper, reopened two files on women who had been attacked in 1975: Mrs Anna Patricia Rogulski of Keighley and Mrs Olive Smelt of Halifax. The attack on the latter especially seemed to have been made by the Ripper before he killed Wilma McCann in October 1975.

Mrs Anna Patricia Rogulski, a 34-year-old housewife, of Highfield Lane, Keighley, was found with severe head injuries behind the Ritz cinema at 2 a.m. on 5 July, 1975. She had been struck over the head with a blunt instrument in an alleyway off North Queen Street and there were injuries to her body similar to those of later murder victims. Policewomen waited at Mrs Rogulski's bedside, but she told them that she had been attacked from behind and could not give any description of her attacker.

Mrs Olive Smelt, 46-year-old mother of three children who worked as an office cleaner for a firm of solicitors in Halifax, was sadistically attacked near her home in Woodside Mount, Boothtown, the other side of town from where Josephine Whitaker was to be murdered. She had been beaten over the head and face, and her buttocks had been slashed. She was left for dead with her skull fractured in two places. Later her husband, Harry Smelt, said he thought a young man who was courting nearby put his car lights on, and that disturbed the Ripper.

Mrs Smelt had met a girl-friend in Halifax on the night of 15 August, 1975 for a Friday evening drink, and two more friends had given her a lift to the top of her street. In September 1978, when asked to try and recall what happened she told a reporter of the *Halifax Evening Courier*: 'I was near the top of the road when a man in his 30s and casually dressed said: "Weather's letting us down, isn't it?" ' He then smashed her over the head twice and cut her buttocks and back. She was not sexually attacked and she was not robbed, even though she was carrying money at the time. She was taken to her house and then to Halifax Infirmary and later to Leeds Infirmary where she spent ten days. Her husband, who was shown the x-rays, said his wife's skull 'looked like a smashed coconut'.

Mr Smelt, who had put his young son Stephen, aged 9, to bed and had watched the Marcus Nelson Murders on TV that night, was called out soon after midnight from the house, and later told his daughters Linda, aged 25, and Julie, aged 15, that he thought the police suspected him.

Police were given a description of the man who spoke to someone else in the area shortly before the attack. He was aged about 30, 5 ft 10 ins tall, slightly built and had dark hair with some beard or growth on his face and spoke with a 'foreign accent'. Three days after the midnight attack police began seeking a man seen running along Woodside View. He was wearing dark clothing, had collar-length hair, was aged between 30 and 35, and was 5 ft 6 ins to 5 ft 8 ins in height.

Mrs Smelt was lucky to survive; twelve others were to be less fortunate.

*

Morley is a proud town – too proud, some say, for its own good. It has lain across the high ridge of land which carries the main Bradford–Wakefield road for over one and a half thousand years, setting itself up as a target successively for invading Danes, the marauding Scots of Wallace and Robert the Bruce, Flemish weavers and finally the wool barons of the nineteenth century. Long before the Norman Conquest it was the centre of one of West Yorkshire's eleven wapentakes – rallying points to which Saxon leaders would come to touch spears with their chief as a token of allegiance.

In the 1950s Morley became briefly famous for having more television sets than household baths, but its pork pies are widely acknowledged to be the best in the world. It has bred its share of famous and infamous sons: one was Herbert Henry Asquith who, as Home Secretary, investigated, with the Troup Committee, Britain's first fingerprint system, and as Prime Minister carried the British Empire into the First World War. Another was Donald Neilson, who made world headlines as the 'Black Panther' before being caught and jailed for life in 1976 for killing heiress Leslie Whittle and three post office employees.

All these events Morley has taken in its stride, but it is the town's high and mighty physical position which brings trouble every winter with knife-edged gales which whip across from the Pennines and slice through the exposed buildings on the ridge, rattling windows, toppling chimneys, and scattering slates like playing cards. On the night of Sunday, 18 January, 1976 the gales struck for the first time in the New Year. They swept frozen rain down through the town centre and along the steep road that runs through the village of Churwell into the city of Leeds.

Lying in bed in his neat, red brick house in Harwill Avenue, Churwell, retired newsagent George White heard the clatter as several sections of his roof lifted from their pinnings and skittered down into the gutter. As supplier of newspapers and magazines to the village for over twenty years, George knew every family in Churwell. 'A job for Sydney Jackson,' he thought irritably before rolling over and seeking sleep.

The following morning the winds had not abated. George rang Jackson, the local roofing expert, at his home and workshop at Back Green, the older part of the village.

'Right, George,' said Jackson. 'I'll send Emily down with the gear on her way to take the kids to school.'

Sydney Jackson was a pale, slight man, but industrious, known and respected for his dedication to his little one-man business; Yorkshiremen admire 'hard grafters'. But he had one odd quirk: Sydney Jackson did not like to drive. Instead his wife Emily, who also acted as secretary and book-keeper, delivered her husband and his tools and materials to each job, helping unload the truck and sometimes even lending a hand with the work. Mrs Jackson was, in the local parlance, 'a strapping, well set up lass'.

The Jacksons were not from 'Churrill' as the natives pronounce the name of their village. To be a 'Churrillite' proper one's grandparents need to have been born in the place. Sydney Jackson was a native of Armley, a suburb of Leeds noted for its top security jail, while his wife came from the mining village of Hemsworth. They had lived in another Leeds suburb, Holbeck, until moving to their current address seven years previously. But even then they made little attempt to join the life of their adopted village, mixing only infrequently with the regulars at the three pubs – the Commercial, the Fleece, and the New Inn – known colloquially as the Top Hole, Middle Hole, and Bottom Hole, from their geographical location on Churwell Hill. Instead, the Jacksons set off to drink at either the Crystal Palace, Holbeck, or in one of the Leeds city pubs, Mrs Jackson driving the battered van.

The morning of Monday, 19 January dawned clear and cold. The rain had stopped, but the wind still drew tatters of cloud across the wintry blue sky. At a quarter to nine

George White heard the van pull up outside and opened his front door. Emily Jackson, a sturdy, dark-haired woman, handsome in an almost masculine way, was getting down from the cab. From the passenger side two children hopped down – her ten-year-old son Christopher and Angela, aged eight.

'By but it's a cold 'un this morning,' said George, rubbing his hands briskly. Mrs Jackson nodded and smiled. 'Now you go carefully across that road,' she called to her children. 'Just think on!'

Already the youngsters were skipping up the avenue towards School Street, named after the grey stone Victorian building which stood on the far side. If there was an extra urgency in the maternal admonition, George White understood it. Five years previously, tragedy had struck the Jackson family when their elder son Derek had fallen head first from his bedroom window and died on the pavement below. Some said that it was to forget the horror of that incident that the Jacksons went out drinking so often. But whatever the family problems, the two youngest were neat and well groomed, and the oldest surviving son, eighteen-year-old Neil, had turned out to be a fine young man who helped his parents with their business.

George White helped Mrs Jackson unload a pile of roofing slates from the back of the van, and together they man-handled one of two extension ladders from the roof rack. Telling George that her husband would be along later in the day to carry out the repairs, Emily Jackson climbed back into her cab and drove off. George White never saw Emily Jackson again.

As far as is known, Sydney and Emily Jackson did not go out on that Monday evening. The past month had, after all, been a hectic one for them. At Christmas they had visited Emily's aunt at the Fairfield Estate in Bramley, Leeds, for a family party which had straggled on for several days. They had seen the New Year in with old friends and neighbours at the Crystal Palace, before going on to another jovial gathering which had lasted well into the morning of New Year's Day. And this had been only the beginning; each evening had found the Jacksons in one merry group or another, sometimes in pubs, sometimes in private houses, keeping out the winter chills with booze and bonhomie. It was a familiar part of the couple's life together.

Sydney had met Emily for the first time twenty-four years previously, when he was twenty-one and she was nineteen, and they had married the following year. That was 1953, the year of the coronation of Queen Elizabeth II, a year of patriotic flag waving and street parties. It was also the year in which John Reginald Halliday Christie, the Yorkshire born sex killer, went to the gallows for the murder of eight women in London's Notting Hill.

True, they had marital difficulties. In the mid-fifties Emily walked out on her husband but returned to him eighteen months later, and their marriage carried on much as before. Even the death of their son Derek only seemed to draw them closer together – but it does seem to have intensified their drinking sprees. As Sydney was later to recall: 'When that happened we decided that life was too short. We would live for today, and not bother about the future. Our life together was happy and we both believed in having a good time . . . in having fun while we could.'

But there was a dark side to these days of wine and roses – a side of which none of the Churwell villagers was aware. The fact was that the Leeds police knew Emily Jackson to be a prostitute, though she had no convictions for soliciting. As was later established, her regular 'beat' was similar to that of Wilma McCann, whom she almost certainly knew, but her method differed in one important respect from most other Leeds street women. Emily Jackson cruised the Chapeltown Road–Sheepscar area at the wheel of her husband's blue van, usually after dropping him off at a public house. When her evening's work was over, she would pick him up and take him back to respectable Churwell. Perhaps the van lent her a sense of security but if it did it was to prove tragically false.

By 5.30 on the afternoon of Tuesday, 20 January, Jackson's roofing work was over for the day – a busy day because of the continuing windy weather. Christopher and Angela were home from school and fed, and had settled down to an evening's television before bed. Emily Jackson applied her make-up carefully, and then changed from her day wear into a skirt, a tight blue and white striped sweater and sling-back shoes. Over the sweater she donned a white cardigan, as added protection against the cold night air, and finally put on a blue, green and red checked overcoat. Despite her dumpy five foot six inch frame and her squarish jaw, her brown hair was smartly cut and her rather small eyes were enlarged with mascara. She took a last look at herself in the bedroom mirror before calling to her husband, 'I'm ready, Syd.' The wind buffeted the van as they rolled down Churwell Hill, but once into the suburbs of Leeds they were protected by the buildings. The lights of Briggate and Boar Lane shone brightly as they drove past the great covered market complex, a huge nineteenth-century edifice of cast iron, granite, and glass, smelling of fish, sawdust and old vegetables. Traffic lights on the modern overhead gantries guided them over the Headrow and on towards Roundhay Road and their favourite venue, the Gaiety public house, where well-dressed West Indians mingle with Poles, Irishmen, Jews – all representative of successive waves of immigration into the city – as well as with Yorkshiremen and women. The music ranges from country and western to reggae, from disco to soft ballads. And the jokes of the comedians tend to fall rather curiously into three classes – nostalgia for the 'bad old days', sexism, and racism.

'Me mam and dad were running for t'air-raid shelter

when she said she'd forgotten her false teeth. "They're droppin' bombs not bloody pork pies," he says.'

'I'm glad to see suspender belts comin' back. Feller who invented tights must have invented this one way system out here – you can't get into them buggers either.'

'We're int' Common Market now with all these krauts and frogs. Frogs lasted longer int' World Cup than they did int'war.'

Oddly the pejorative words such as 'nigger' and 'Paki' which tend to grate on southern ears are used here easily and almost, one might say, with affection. The West Indians laugh hugely and then tell their 'Irish' jokes to Irishmen. The hubbub of talk and laughter is constant beneath the blue folds of cigarette smoke.

The Jacksons parked their van in the Gaiety car park at about ten minutes to six and walked into the already lively atmosphere. Sydney bought drinks, and they stood for a while talking at the bar. At ten past six, Emily emptied her glass of lager and threaded her way out again into the car park towards her husband's van. Some time between then and 10.30 p.m. the blue Commer van was driven from the car park – presumably by Emily – and it was back there before dawn the following day. By that time Emily was incapable of any action. At 6.30 p.m. fellow street walkers saw her talking to a character they knew as 'Ginger' in the Spencer Place area of Chapeltown. Other reports, though unconfirmed, had Emily travelling the streets later in the evening.

At 10.30 p.m. Sydney Jackson went to the Gaiety car park and scanned the darkness for the familiar van. It was not there. Whether he thought she had gone without him or to another bar he never subsequently made clear. But he telephoned a taxi which took him home to Churwell.

What is certain is that somewhere in the area a man sat in a darkened car, away from the street lights, perhaps in one of the many side turnings off Sheepscar or North

Street or Chapeltown Road. On such a night the car heater would have been on, the engine quietly turning over in neutral, the steamed-up windscreen needing a wipe from time to time. He was a patient man, deeply cunning. He was waiting for someone like Emily Jackson. A loose woman. A prostitute he could batter to death.

A curious policeman would not have noticed anything unusual about this working man in his old 'banger' however. Even a search would have revealed only the tools of his trade – spanners, wrenches, files perhaps, screwdrivers and hammers, as well as motorists' gear such as a jack and tyre levers. But it was by the marks of some of these tools that detectives were later to recognize the trademark of the strange motorist – the Yorkshire Ripper.

In the early dawn light of Wednesday, 21 January, a workman picked his way through the shadows of a 'ginnel' – a narrow passageway – which led from Manor Street to Roundhay Road. The whole area was derelict, awaiting demolition. Opposite, Roundhay Road School had been empty for almost a year. Tufts of rank grass grew between the cobbles, and urban litter – old bottles, tin cans, and splintered wood – made him pick his way carefully in the half darkness. To his left was a cul-de-sac which ran back thirty feet into inky shadow; on the right-hand side stood a partly burned-out ruin, windows empty, doors agape. Something bulky and dark on the pavement by this building caught the workman's attention. He approached, peered down.

What he saw sent him blundering out through the ginnel and into Roundhay Road, looking around wildly for a telephone kiosk. Breathlessly he found one near the junction of Sheepscar and North Street, flung open the door and dialled 999.

The officers manning the patrol car which answered the telephone call were fully aware of the McCann killing of the previous year, in all its grisly details. One glance had them radioing police headquarters, and within minutes Detective Chief Superintendent Dennis Hoban was on his way with the police surgeon. As the sky lightened, uniformed men cordoned off the area while the senior officer and his aides stood in the textbook positions advocated at detective training schools – 'hands in pockets, eyes open, mouth shut' – watching the surgeon begin his first, tentative examination.

Emily Jackson lay sprawled face downwards, her stained overcoat over her, her brown hair black with dried blood. Her skirt and lower underwear were still in position, but the cardigan and striped sweater had been removed and lay nearby with her shoes and tan handbag. Apart from the head wounds, she had been stabbed fifty times, after the initial rain of blows to her head had felled her some yards away from where the body was lying. Marks on the ground showed how the killer had dragged her to the spot, probably before making his last, frenzied assault. The contents of her handbag were intact, and from them detectives learned Emily's name and address. Police cars sped up the hill to Churwell, for at this stage Sydney Jackson had to be 'number one in the frame' – the chief suspect, as police jargon had it.

Shortly after nine o'clock that morning Mrs Audrey Thorpe, part owner of a firm of building contractors, who lived two doors away from the Jacksons answered an urgent knocking at her front door. She knew Sydney Jackson well, not only as a neighbour but because of their mutual business interests – he frequently helped her on roofing jobs. But the figure confronting her when she opened the door was very different to the happy-go-lucky man who had 'lived for the moment'. His face was ashen, his hair in disarray. It took Jackson some seconds before he got out the words. 'Will you . . . will you look after

Christopher and Angela for me if they're home from school before I get back?' he stammered. 'Emily . . . Emily's had an accident.' 'When I asked him how she was and what had happened,' Mrs Thorpe was to recall later, 'he was so upset he couldn't tell me what was wrong. He couldn't talk at all.'

For Sydney Jackson it was the beginning of a gruelling day: first the formal identification of his wife's body and then a grilling at Chapeltown police headquarters which lasted until 11.30 p.m. and covered all aspects of his life with Emily Jackson, their friends, business associates, clients, regular haunts. For over 150 hand-picked policemen it was the beginning of an equally gruelling investigation: an extension, for most of them, of the investigation they had begun into the slaughter of Wilma McCann in the same neighbourhood just under four months previously.

Even as Mrs Jackson's body – the head and hands swathed in protective polythene bags – was lifted carefully on to a stretcher for transportation to the city mortuary, a dozen men on hands and knees began searching the ginnel and cul-de-sac in which she had died, painstakingly picking their way through the coarse grass, placing any likely clue – a cigarette butt, scrap of paper, blood-splashed pebble – into individual envelopes for minute examination later.

Every stage of the hunt at the site was recorded by police photographers, some with Polaroid cameras for immediate comparison purposes; and under a tent erected over the stretch of pavement on which the body had lain, forensic scientists from Wetherby carefully measured the blood stains and recorded each mark on a squared, graph-paper chart. Blood splashes, smears, and blobs were checked for the direction and the height from which they had fallen. Exclamation-shaped splashes told the examiner a great deal more than blobs, which are usually the result of blood falling vertically, while smears had their own significance –

the dragging of the body and movement of the limbs of the victim after attack. A sample of every stain found was also scraped on to a glass microscope slide for laboratory comparison later.

Meanwhile, in the car park of the Gaiety pub a few hundred yards away, Emily Jackson's blue Commer van with its BNK953K registration number had been found. This presented Mr Hoban with a new angle to ponder. The van was not there at 10.30 p.m. the previous evening, when last orders were called, and the landlord had not seen it while locking up an hour or so later. Therefore someone had driven it back during the early hours of the morning – but who? Was it Emily Jackson herself who had parked the vehicle before going out again to prowl the streets on foot, or had she picked up her assailant in the van and driven him unwittingly to the place of her death, leaving him afterwards to coolly replace the vehicle in the car park? Why should he have bothered? In all probability the nocturnal killer had that kind of audacity, and it was towards this theory that Mr Hoban leaned when he called his first press conference early that afternoon at Chapeltown police headquarters.

The first, routine morning call to the police station had given reporters an indication that the man who had killed Wilma McCann had probably struck again, and the small, smoke-filled room was packed with the local press and with area representatives of national newspapers. Each was handed a blown up photograph of the dead woman, taken from a snapshot provided by her husband. Already the police community relations department were distributing even bigger enlargements for posting throughout the Leeds area, with her name and details of her last known movements, headed by a block capital line: HAVE YOU SEEN THIS WOMAN? At busy junctions in the Roundhay Road area, police vans bearing the same gigantic poster on their sides stood prominently by the roadside, their crews stopping passers by and filing reports of their movements.

Meanwhile that morning in the wash room adjoining the mortuary of Leeds General Infirmary, Professor David Gee was removing his heavy yellow rubber apron and gum boots, stripping off his surgical gloves and cap, and mentally turning over the results of the post-mortem examination he had just performed in the next room. As one mortuary technician closed the body cavity of Mrs Jackson's corpse, another was busy labelling samples of tissue and blood prior to sending them by fast car to the Wetherby forensic laboratory for examination. But Professor Gee was sure of one fact already: the savage battering which the dead woman had undergone, the shattered skull, lacerated scalp and stab wounds to her upper body, was identical in so many ways to those he had seen on Wilma McCann months before that the similarities could not be coincidental. That evening his confidential report was in the hands of Dennis Hoban.

As night fell again over the windy city, the gales and the fear swept the streets clear of almost everyone except policemen. People were petrified, mothers imagined the horrors of it happening to their own daughters and dreaded the thought of them walking alone at night. Nurses in particular feared the Ripper because of the late hours that shift changeovers take place. Generators hummed over the police check points, flooding the scene with harsh white lights as the officers continued their monotonous but vital task of stopping cars and pedestrians. 'What were your movements between six o'clock last night and seven this morning? Were you in this area? Did you see any parked vehicles? What were they like?'

There is little of his Scotland Yard counterpart's stridency about the average Yorkshire copper. Even his accent is softer, more persuasive, inviting confidence. 'I see, love. And what was this feller you saw like? Can you remember the colour of his hair? Aye, well it is dark around here these nights. Was he wearing an overcoat do you know? . . .'

Two or three locals remembered a blue, 'L' registered Thames van parked near a food warehouse in Roundhay Road at 3.45 a.m. that morning. Later the police were to appeal for the driver to come forward to be eliminated from their inquiries – yet another line of questioning which was to peter out disappointingly. Some girls told policemen of their fears and one 22-year-old girl, known to the law as an amateur prostitute, was stopped while hurrying home to her flat. 'Since this killing today I've decided to give up the game,' she said fervently. 'It's getting too frightening. Only at Christmas I had my nose broken by a man in the street. He just walked up to me and said "how's business" and then punched me in the face. I've been dead scared ever since and this murder has clinched it.'

Another more hardened woman of 34 who had operated in the area for over fifteen years spoke for many of her colleagues: 'Young or old, we're all scared stiff. We're all keeping off the streets as much as possible.'

Even respectable women were not immune from the terror that walked by night. One rang the police station to complain that her 16- and 14-year-old daughters were regularly accosted while walking home through Chapeltown in their school uniforms. Whatever other result the murders of McCann and Jackson might have, they were already highlighting the plight of the majority of respectable, largely immigrant, residents who suffered because of the area's red light reputation.

At 11.30 p.m. Sydney Jackson, red eyed and wan, was driven home to Churwell in a police car – home to an empty house. His three children had gone to stay with their mother's sister in the village of Old Farnley a mile away across the fields. The two youngest, Christopher and Angela, still did not know their mother was dead and neither their aunt nor their father had had the heart to tell them.

All through the night, the lights burned at Chapeltown police headquarters, where an incident room had been set up and functioning for almost twelve hours now. Wall charts pinpointing the movements or reported sightings of cars and pedestrians at quarter-of-an-hour intervals during the appropriate period of time were amended as new information came in. Telephones shrilled ceaselessly. Ashtrays filled up. Carton after carton of hot tea, watery coffee and thick, sweet chocolate were drunk and tossed empty into waste bins. Officers queueing for use of the limited number of typewriters eased their ties and scratched stubbly chins.

Dennis Hoban, after a briefly snatched rest period, began preparing his morning briefing. The most important item on the agenda was to be the methodical checking of an address book taken from the Jackson home. One of the last entries in it was George White's hastily scribbled name and address. The book was to prove another disappointment: it was a list of clients, true – but clients who had used Sydney Jackson's services as a roofing specialist, not his wife's services as a prostitute.

Some detectives were assigned to 'pub duty' – mingling with the lunchtime crowds at the Gaiety and other houses in the area. Tact, however, was to be their watchword: each subject for interview was unostentatiously approached and quietly shown a warrant card, asked to step outside for a word. Several volunteered to accompany the policemen to Chapeltown station for further inquiries to be made. All proved negative.

On Friday, 23 January the police station's conference room was crowded with reporters from local and national newspapers. Mr Hoban had to elbow his way through to the slightly raised rostrum at the far end, but silence fell as soon as he appeared. Solemnly he told the pressmen that Mrs Jackson had been 'in the habit of patrolling the streets of Chapeltown for the purposes of prostitution'. Yes, he confirmed, the similarities between the death of Mrs Jackson and that of Wilma McCann were unmistakable. The police were also looking again at the file on the unsolved murder of a Mrs Mary Judge, aged 43, who had been found battered to death six years previously on waste land near Leeds Parish Church.

'All three women,' said Mr Hoban, 'followed a similar pattern of life, visiting pubs and clubs as prostitutes, although the Jackson and McCann killings are the only ones definitely linked. Besides her head wounds,' he went on, 'Mrs Jackson was stabbed fifty times. In both cases the obvious deep-seated hatred of prostitutes manifested itself in the many stab wounds. While this man, who shows every sign of being a psychopath, is at large, no prostitute is safe.'

Mr Hoban told the reporters that more than a hundred Task Force officers were searching the area for clues.

We have also had the help of a number of girls who worked in the area as prostitutes, and I appeal for others to come forward. Their information so far has been helpful, and we are following up several lines of inquiry. We have established that Mrs Jackson's method of soliciting was to drive around in her husband's blue Commer van and pick up clients. Sometimes she would leave the van in the Gaiety car park, and go with clients in their own cars, when they would drive to some secluded place for sex, It was probably on one of these excursions that she met her killer.

Mr Hoban paused before he delivered his next sentence. 'I can not stress strongly enough,' he said, 'that it is vital that we catch this brutal killer before he brings tragedy to another family.'

The *Evening Post* arrived at Churwell's newspaper shop – George White's business before he sold it – at 5.30 p.m.

The story of Emily Jackson's murder was front page news, and there was a brisker trade than usual from villagers. Sydney Jackson was to tell reporters later that he felt, during that first day, that Churrillites would think he was responsible for the murder. The thought never seems to have entered their heads. It was the fact of his wife's 'second profession' which surprised them.

'Never in a hundred years would I have thought Emily Jackson was on the game,' said George Radnall, landlord of the Commercial – the Top Hole – in which the couple had occasionally gone drinking. The thought was echoed by every one in the other two village pubs.

In the old people's shelter at the top of Old Road which served as a memorial to the men of the village who died in the First World War, some pensioners recalled a legendary prostitute of the village: Annie Houghty, an Irishwoman who, during the early 1940s, had supplemented the income she got from selling scouring stone gathered from the railway cutting, by prostitution. Annie Houghty too had died alone, and in as brutal a fashion as Emily Jackson; her clog had caught under the railway line, and before she could free it she was struck by a Leeds–Manchester express. Within months, the village kids had evolved a 'skipping' rhyme about the event:

Annie on the railway, picking up stones,
Down came an engine and broke her little bones.
Oh, said Annie, that's not fair,
Ah, said the engine, I don't care.

chapter five

The year of 1977 was to be the Yorkshire Ripper's bloodiest. Four more women were to die and two others to be brutally assaulted. Until the last attack in that year, when he crossed the Pennines into Lancashire, the brunt of the investigation into this man's vengeance was borne by the Yorkshire police.

The fourth murdered victim, 28-year-old Mrs Irene Richardson, a native of Glasgow, was, in the words of Police Inspector Roy Spencer of Millgarth police headquarters, Leeds, 'one of the saddest cases of all', because she was simply a woman who had fallen on hard times, was hanging around the street corners of Chapeltown, and was mistaken for a prostitute by the Ripper.

Irene Richardson, mother of two daughters aged four and five, who lived with foster-parents, was found by a jogger, battered and stabbed to death in Soldiers' Field, Roundhay Park, Leeds, at 7.50 a.m. on a bright, crisp, sunny morning, Sunday, 6 February, 1977. Her throat had been cut. She had not been sexually assaulted, her handbag with money in it was lying nearby, and her watch was still ticking on her wrist.

On Saturday, 22 January, 1977 Irene Richardson should have gone to Leeds Register Office to meet the man she had been seeing during the three months she had lived in Leeds. He was Stephen Bray, a former seaman, chef, night-club doorman and gaolbird. Neither had turned up for the wedding for neither had told the other that they were already married. Mrs Richardson had a husband, Mr George Biggart Richardson, a plasterer living in Blackpool, and Bray, who was on the run from Lancaster Gaol where he was serving a four-year sentence for theft, had a wife in Hull.

During the two weeks between the date fixed for their

wedding and the night of the murder, 5 February, Irene Richardson and Stephen Bray had split up and he had gone to Ireland and then to London, where he was interviewed by police and later put into Armley Gaol, Leeds.

Detective Chief Superintendent James Hobson, head of Leeds CID in charge of the murder hunt, was another highly experienced detective who had been commended twelve times during his service and who had been involved in one of the most remarkable police operations in Britain – the voluntary fingerprinting of 25,000 people during the inquiry into the murder of Leeds shopkeeper Annie Blenkarn. He told reporters:

In the last ten days of her life, Irene Richardson was wandering about, without accommodation, practically penniless and hanging about street corners in the Chapeltown area. It may well be that she was mistaken for a prostitute because she had nowhere to go. It is probable that she accepted a lift to Roundhay and was killed there. She got on well with the people she lived next to in rooming houses at four or five different addresses in Leeds. She seems to have been a jovial type of person and there is more and more evidence that she was trying to get work. Some of her friends, however, told the police that Irene, who had been working as a chambermaid, was depressed.

Mrs Richardson had not been drawing Social Security. She was last seen alive at 11.15 p.m. on Saturday, 5 February in Cowper Street where she had had a room and she said she was going to Tiffany's club, where Stephen Bray had worked as a doorman before he left for Ireland. She had tried to make herself look as attractive as possible to go to the club, and had put on a blue and white checked blouse, brown cardigan, yellow jacket and skirt, an imitation suede coat with fur trimmings and brown, calf-length boots. She had combed her shoulder-length brown hair carefully and put on some bangles. She made herself up and dressed carefully and smartly because the club was frequented by well-dressed people. The advertisements for Tiffany's specified 'No denims', and called itself: 'Supper Disco. Non-stop dancing 8 p.m. to 1 a.m. Late Bar. Lots of give-aways – Free T-shirts and albums.'

During that half-hour gap between Mrs Richardson leaving the rooming house in Cowper Street (now replaced by a new block of flats) and the time of death given by Professor Gee, she was picked up by the Ripper and driven to Soldiers' Field, so-called because British Army men had camped on the field prior to going overseas in the First World War. It is only a few minutes drive away. In Round-hay Road, which leads to the park, there is a flash of pastel shades in the streets of immigrant-occupied houses, some with purple drainpipes, there is the Habib Bank of Pakistan and an Asian estate agent and property dealer. On the right of Soldiers' Field is Prince's Avenue with a double row of plane trees on the left and a single row on the right. To the right of that are the grand mansions of West Avenue, home of TV celebrity Jimmy Savile, and to the left is the peaceful Old Park Road, with more detached mansions overlooking the cricket ground.

In the half dark of that Sunday morning in February, Mr John Bolton, a 46-year-old accountant, of Gledhow Lane, Leeds, was jogging over the wet grass when he saw the body of Irene Richardson in the shadow of the sports pavilion. He trotted over and said: 'Hello. What's the matter?' Then he realized that there could be no reply from the figure on the grass that he had stumbled on during his pre-breakfast run.

I could see it was a woman lying on her side. Her face was turned down towards the grass and covered by her hair. I brushed the hair to one side and then I saw the blood on her neck and her eyes were glazed and staring. She was obviously dead, so I ran to one of the houses and called the police.

During the next three months 11,000 people were interviewed by the police team led by Mr Hobson, who saw
very little of his wife and only daughter during the intensive
hunt that followed the murder in Roundhay Park. He told
Chris Bye of the *Evening Post*:

One hundred and twenty men are working on the murders.
We are still interviewing prostitutes in the Chapeltown area
and asking them about any man who may have been violent
towards them. If we can get a number of descriptions we can
put them together and get some sort of an idea of the man
we're looking for. We are also following up a possible link
with another similar type of murder in Preston in November
1975 [Joan Harrison] when a prostitute was found stabbed to
death in the town centre. The fact that all three women –
McCann, Jackson, Richardson – were picked up in the same
area, the fact that two of them were found dead on playing
fields, and the fact that the injuries are very similar, makes a
link between them. Mrs Richardson was not a known
prostitute but we know she was depressed. She could have gone
in a car with a man as a 'punter' after she had visited Tiffany's.
We are still trying to trace her movements that night.

On 10 February, 1977 Mr Hobson and detectives working
on the McCann–Jackson–Richardson murders studied a
file on 20-year-old Marcella Claxton who had been attacked
and beaten unconscious by a man on Soldiers' Field not
far from the spot where Richardson's body was found.
This happened on 9 May, 1976 after she had accepted a
lift in a large white car in Chapeltown. After the attack she
went into hiding in the Gathorne area of Chapeltown. She
said:

I am still in fear of my life. I think I can identify him, and he
must know that. I had been to a party and I was drunk. I was
on my way home when a man in a white car stopped to give
me a lift. He was well spoken and smartly dressed and said he
did not live in Leeds. He took me to the fields and ordered me
to strip. I said 'No' and then he started to beat me. I don't

62

know what he hit me with. I was in hospital for several days and I needed fifty stitches in the head. Since then I have seen the police several times to try and help them to find this man.

She described her attacker as between 25 and 35, 5 ft 9 ins tall, driving a large white four-door car with red upholstery. He was very well spoken, wore a plain ring on his right hand and was of fattish build. He also had podgy hands. Mr Hobson said after talking to Marcella Claxton and examining the file carefully: 'We have an open mind on this girl's story.' But Marcella Claxton is playing safe and living at a secret address.

Bradford is arguably the wealthiest city in Yorkshire, a county often referred to as the 'Texas of England' – although Yorkshiremen prefer to call Texas the 'Yorkshire of the United States'. Its fortunes were founded on wool and customers from all over the world still flock to buy Bradford-woven worsteds, the best suiting cloths that money can buy. In the town's heyday between the two world wars there were said to be more millionaire members of the Bradford Wool Exchange than all the millionaire oilmen and cattle barons of Texas put together.

There is an enigma about the average Bradfordian's character which is not easily resolved. He will speak with pride of novelists J. B. Priestley and John Braine, painter David Hockney and nineteenth-century composer Frederick Delius, all born in the city, but he will also point out with mordant delight that three top hangmen, James Berry and Harry and Albert Pierrepoint, were native sons. There is a bluntness about him which sometimes amounts to the boorish – particularly when faced with anything that smacks of pomposity or 'putting on airs and graces'.

An old story tells of a famous Bradford wool magnate striding into the elegantly plush bar of the Victoria hotel in brown boots and flat cap. The sleek barman glided towards him and asked: 'Yes sir? And what is your pleasure?'

'Fuckin' and rattin',' came the reply. 'What's thine?'

Tripe and udder – the steam-cleaned linings of a cow's stomach and milk sac, eaten raw and cold with vinegar, pepper, salt and mustard sauce – is a staple delicacy of Bradford. So are the shiny black-puddings made of dried blood and meal, hot pork pies with 'mushy' peas and the rich, treacle-and-ginger cake known as 'parkin'. The butcher's shops, haberdashers, baker's shops which sprawl down the steep hill towards the city centre exude an air of stolid tradition and more than a whiff of nostalgia.

Modern trends are treated by the older citizens with amusement and vague contempt. Outside one of the city's only 'sex shops' – sited, appropriately enough, in Hustlergate – an old man cast a disdainful eye over the goods on show. 'Do folk need all this stuff nowadays, just to do what used to come natural?' he asked.

Approach the city centre from the north west suburb of Shipley, however, and the new Bradford, a product of the last thirty-odd years, becomes apparent. The Manningham area begins about a mile and a half from the city's main commercial centre, a series of stone-built Victorian and Edwardian villas set in gardens fringed with rhododendrons, laburnum, and privet hedges. Once the homes of the smaller businessmen, they are now the business premises of private dentists, management consultants, architects and insurance brokers and some have become respectable hotels with names like 'Balmoral' and 'Blenheim'.

A mile from the city's hub, the main road called Manningham Lane undergoes an abrupt change of character. The freshly cleaned white stone is replaced by buildings still bearing the soot stains of the area's woollen manufacturing heyday, though the woodwork on shops and houses is brightly painted in pastel shades of pinks, blues and greens. Since the break-up of the British Empire, Bradford has become a major centre for immigration and in 1979, out of the area's total estimated population of 465,000, around 47,000 were of Pakistan, Bangladesh or Indian origin, while a further 5,000 came from the West Indies.

The new Bradfordians, particularly those from Asia, would almost certainly meet with the grudging approval of those nineteenth-century pioneer wool men who built their fortunes from 'hard graft' and shrewd business sense, for the immigrants lost little time in setting up their own bustling community of Manningham Lane–Lumb Lane–Oak Lane. In the mid-1970s, Mr Mohammed Saeed Khan, who ran a business consultancy for his fellow immigrants, told a reporter that by his calculations 500 Asian businesses were thriving in the area, offering everything from saris to Oriental spices.

The Asian influx has made a major difference to the eating habits of the more adventurous members of the white community and many travel to Lumb Lane to sample tandoori dishes, bhajis, biryanis, kebabs and pappadoms, along with sticky delicacies like Royal Halwa, a green fudge stuffed with pistachio nuts. But only a handful of whites venture into the pubs of Lumb Lane – disco-reggae pubs such as the Queens, the Flying Dutchman and the Perseverence – which are packed most evenings with black and brown faces.

To those who know the Asian community there is a curious dichotomy here. Almost a hundred per cent of the original Pakistani and Indian settlers were Moslems and there are still packed prayer meetings, at the Markazi Jamiyat Tagighul-ul-Islam – better known to the whites as the Southfield Square Mosque – which was converted from two terraced houses some years ago. The Moslem faith is still strong enough to pay for a new mosque, the Markazi Jamiyat Ahl-E-Hadith, which is soon to be built opposite the Perseverance pub at a cost of many thousands of pounds. Yet, slowly but surely, attitudes are changing, particularly among young immigrants and Bradford-born Asians. As one Karachi-born lawyer explained, ninety-five per cent of the immigrants are country people, peasants who jet in almost directly from primitive villages and face exactly the same difficulties in Yorkshire as they would if they moved to Bombay or Delhi, for instance.

In Pakistan, drinking, gambling and associating with unmarried women outside the bounds of purdah are still matters for the criminal courts, while in Bradford young Asians suddenly feel free to indulge in all these activities. Even some of their own herbalists emphasize the western attitude to sex, selling deer musk from Nepal and African rhino horn as aphrodisiacs, alongside contraceptives and 'virility creams'.

The results are seen almost nightly by Mrs Audrey Naylor, who runs the Perseverance public house. Mrs Naylor is a pleasant woman who still speaks with a trace of the Devon accent she brought with her to Yorkshire when her Bradford-born husband took the pub in 1946. Since his death several years ago she has been the landlady, with an ever present 'body guard' of her coloured regulars to protect her should trouble start. In fact the majority of customers in Mrs Naylor's pub are neither violent nor prostitutes; the only regular breakages are suffered by her bakelite dominoes. The West Indians and Pakistanis who avidly play the game every night have a habit of banging them down on the table as a sign of victory. In thirteen years she has had to buy a total of 139 sets. In partial recompense she is often invited for a free meal at one of the nearby cafés or clubs; her favourite is the Young Lions Club around the corner which boasts an excellent menu of chillis, chicken fried West Indian style, and spiced rice.

Some of the good-time girls – both locals and visitors to Bradford – do slip into Mrs Naylor's saloon bar in the early evenings. They sit in pairs as a rule, making a glass of lager last until the rich young Pakistanis, usually shy and quietly spoken young men, come in. Offered a drink, the girls invariably ask for a large scotch or gin and orange before leaving with their clients for sex at their flats, or in a parked car, or sometimes in the open air among the bushes of Back Southfield Square – a stone's throw from the mosque.

In the early 1970s a girl in her late twenties began to use the Perseverance and other Lumb Lane pubs. She did not appear to be a local girl; sometimes she called herself Patricia Atkinson, though occasionally she used the name McGee. She was not unattractive, with a slim, slight figure and shoulder-length dark hair and soon she caught the eye of an immigrant worker, Ray Mitra. Mr Mitra apparently had a more westernized outlook than his average country-men; in any case, he risked their disapproval by marrying Patricia Atkinson, whom he nicknamed 'Tina'.

For a few years the couple were fairly happy. Three daughters were born, Judy, Jill and Lisa, and then the 'mixed' marriage turned sour and the Mitras were divorced. Ray Mitra gained custody of the children, partly on the grounds that Tina had already begun sliding back into her old ways – drink, dancing and going with men friends. By the summer of 1976 she had given up all pretence of respect-ability and was openly operating as a prostitute from a small flat she found in Oak Avenue, around the corner from Oak Lane, scene of the busy Sunday morning market which Asian stall-holders compare favourably to Karachi's Bohri Bazaar.

It is doubtful whether Tina Atkinson ever saw or even heard very much of the colourful Sunday gatherings, how-ever. Thursday night is pay night in most Bradford factories and from then until Saturday the money flows. On Friday and Saturday Tina walked around the pubs and clubs of Manningham, her blue jeans tight-fitting and her habitual denim shirt open almost to the waist. She did a brisk trade, largely because of her trim appearance but also because, unlike most local prostitutes, she had a flat of her own.

67

But with Tina Atkinson it was a case of 'never on a Sunday'. When her last client left on Saturday night she locked her door, climbed into bed and stayed there until Sunday evening, when the pubs opened at seven.

Saturday, 23 April, 1977 carried a promise of spring. Few of the new Bradfordians can have known or cared that it was William Shakespeare's birthday or that it was the feast day of their adopted country's patron saint – the red cross of St George fluttering over the distant Town Hall meant little to them. What mattered was the brassy sun in the bright blue sky, which brought out their women in summer saris and which shone on their children's first street cricket games of the year.

Tina Atkinson not only cared little about either Shakespeare or Saint George but the sunlight too held little attraction for her. The bundle of notes she had earned over the busy Easter holiday a fortnight before had almost gone and in the post-holiday period money was scarce and punters would be thin on the ground. Nevertheless she strolled around the streets of Manningham in her faded blue denims and black leather jacket, calling in at pubs to listen to music and sip the odd glass of lager.

As the sky darkened to an inkier blue, Tina eased herself off her bar stool at the Perseverance and made for a pub nearer home – the Carlisle, in Carlisle Road. She was there until 10.15 p.m. and then, three-quarters of an hour before closing time, she left. The evening was warm for the time of the year and Manningham's contingent of street girls was out in force. At about 11.15 one or two of them saw her in St Mary's Road and Church Street, both neighbouring thoroughfares. And then she was gone.

Nineteen hours later, just before Sunday evening opening time, an old friend of Tina's named Robert William Henderson walked down Oak Avenue to the door of number nine and rang the bell. There was no reply. He tried the handle and the front door opened. He walked into the bedroom.

The bedclothes were dishevelled, and beneath a blanket was a huddled bundle. Bob Henderson recognized the body of Tina Atkinson by the black leather jacket and denims, though they were spattered with blood; few other identifying features remained for her head had been beaten out of shape.

Detective Chief Superintendent John Domaille and the surgeon turned up at the cluttered little flat within minutes of Henderson's panic call. Gently the surgeon peeled back the blanket to reveal Tina's corpse and begin his preliminary investigations, as the usual police photographer flashed off shots of the scene from every angle.

There is no such thing as an 'official' police surgeon in Britain, in the sense in which the term is understood in the United States. In the United Kindom the post – in each police division or sub-division – is filled by a general practitioner initially selected by the senior divisional police officer and then approved by the local chief constable. In many cases the term 'police doctor' is preferred, perhaps to indicate that the local man does not as a rule perform the post-mortem examination at the mortuary. He is paid a retainer, plus a fee for each 'call', for checking that the body is indeed dead and for taking an immediate temperature reading, which will later be used as part of the process of establishing time of death.

Tina Atkinson was a known prostitute and for that reason alone the possibility of a sexual motive for her death was a real one; normal temperature-taking procedures – the insertion of a thermometer into the rectum or vagina – had therefore to be ruled out. The alternative method in such cases is to make a small incision through the wall of the abdomen and into the liver, and place the thermometer there. The minute hole is made well away from any injuries the body may have suffered, and is afterwards sealed with a piece of sticking plaster to identify it for what it is.

Despite what detective fiction would have us believe, it

is not always a simple task to establish an exact time of death, because the condition of the corpse depends on a great number of variables, all of which have to be taken into consideration. When death occurs the muscles relax and then begin to stiffen over a period of between ten to twelve hours into the condition of rigor mortis. Over this period the eyes glaze and lose lustre, but certain tissue and molecular activities continue; the medical examiner will often test the pupils with atropine to check on contraction, which will help him in his calculations.

The cooling time of a recently dead body is the main test of death time, although again many considerations have to be made – the state of the weather and atmospheric conditions, the temperature of the room if the corpse is indoors and the state of the corpse itself – fat, thin, muscular, old, young, ill or healthy and so on. The average fall in temperature is about 1° Fahrenheit per hour, increasing slightly as time goes on, the limbs cooling rather more quickly than the main trunk – which is why rectal or liver temperatures are taken as soon as possible.

The surface of a body found indoors will usually be completely cold within eight to twelve hours, but complete cooling of a healthy adult body, particularly one clothed or covered in a blanket, will not reach room temperature for twenty to thirty hours. The formula normally used is 37° Centigrade (the normal body temperature of a living person) minus the rectal or liver temperature of the corpse, multiplied by two, equals the approximate number of hours since death occurred.

After taking a temperature reading, the examiner will check on the presence of hypostasis or post-mortem lividity. When blood circulation ceases the blood drains to the lowest parts of the body, showing through the skin as a purplish stain which is fixed after a period of six to eight hours. At the points where the body has been in contact with the surface on which it lies, however, the skin remains unstained; this means that the medical examiner can tell immediately if the body has been moved after the onset of hypostasis. Sometimes bruising caused before death may be confused with the marks of hypostasis; to differentiate between the two states an incision is made into the centre of the discoloration at the time of the post-mortem. If it is hypostasis only a few oozing capillaries will be noticed, whereas bruising will have caused blood to coagulate under the skin.

The progress of rigor mortis is also carefully noted in establishing time of death. This condition, again beloved of detective fiction writers, is caused, simply speaking, by the coagulation of muscle plasma which tenses and stiffens the muscles in a strict order. First to be affected, about an hour to an hour-and-a-half after death, are the eyelids; after a similar period the jaw muscles become rigid, then the neck, the face, the thorax, the arms, the trunk, and the legs and feet. About thirty-six hours later rigor begins to pass off again in the same order and on the same time scale in which it appeared, starting at the eyelids and ending with the feet.

It was as a result of the surgeon's findings from these calculations that Mr Domaille was able to announce to the press that 33-year-old Tina Atkinson had died shortly after returning to her flat late on Saturday night or early Sunday morning. His own inquiries led him to believe that she had been picked up by a man in a car at about 11.15 p.m. on the Saturday. She had not been raped but she had, he said 'been the victim of a frenzied sexual attack and had been struck many blows about the head'.

But it was the full-scale post-mortem at the hands of Professor Gee and his report on the nature of the wounds which confirmed Mr Domaille in his worst fear – that Tina was not only the fifth known woman to have died at the hands of the Yorkshire Ripper, but that she had achieved the macabre distinction of being his first 'indoor' victim.

Like many of her colleagues on the street Tina had carried an address book, which in her case contained the names of over fifty regular clients. Despite the usual painstaking checks on all these and a massive police inquiry which covered the entire area, with Urdu- and Punjabi-speaking detectives being employed, her killer remains at large.

chapter six

Jayne MacDonald, aged 16, who worked in the shoe department of a supermarket in Leeds, shouted 'Goodnight' to Mr Jack Bransberg, a neighbour who worked with her father on British Rail. She had told him that she was going first to the Astoria Ballroom and then to a disco on Round-hay Road. Jayne always told the Bransbergs where she was going on a Saturday night and it was her habit to telephone them with a message if she was going to stay with a friend as Mr Bransberg would relay the message to her parents, Wilfred and Irene MacDonald in Reginald Terrace, Chapeltown. She went out every Saturday night, either dancing at the Merrion Centre discos or roller skating.

Everyone seems to have liked her. 'She was a smashing girl, with film star good looks, but absolutely unspoilt,' said one neighbour, Mrs Edith Ferguson.

Jayne was known as a happy-go-lucky girl, very close to

her family. The night she left the family home in Reginald Terrace she bent down to kiss her father, near the silver cup on the sideboard she and her brother and sister had bought, inscribed: FOR THE WORLD'S BEST DAD. Her hair was shining, freshly washed and she was glowing with health. Her shoulder-length brown hair flounced against her blue-grey waist-length gaberdine jacket and she wore a blue and white gingham skirt and brown and cream platform shoes to add a little extra to her 5 ft 3 ins height. In her handbag was a letter for her sister in South Africa, Mrs Carol Skorpen, thanking her for an invitation to visit 'before you settle down in Leeds' and telling her about a holiday she was planning in Spain. Carol had not seen her sister Jayne for ten years and Jayne had talked to friends about a future visit.

Saturday, 25 June, 1977 was a warm summer night and as Jayne left to go to the town centre there were already many groups of West Indians on the streets and many parties had been planned for that night. They were night people who liked to stand around and talk into the small hours of the morning after the parties ended.

Jayne had no steady boyfriend then. She had broken off with 18-year-old Steven Martin because, as she told her mother: 'It's getting too serious.' Jayne wanted to stay free a while longer, like her elder sister Janet, who was 19. It was another young man she danced with that night at the Hofbrauhaus in the city centre and he offered to escort her home later.

The Hofbrauhaus was one of Jayne's favourite places. A replica of the Munich *bierkellers*, it is always full of life and songs and young people sit at long wooden tables, drink steins of beer and sing 'The Happy Wanderer' as it is thumped out by a 'German' band, which consists of a Liverpudlian, a Geordie and local lads, wearing *lederhosen* and feathered Tyrolean hats. There are Bavarian and English dishes and a notice at the side of the bandstand says: *Ein Prosit! Ein Prosit! Der Gemütlichkeit*. The youngsters happily swaying to the music of 'Rosamunde' and 'The Happy Wanderer' understand the word *Gemütlichkeit*, a kind of carefree happiness or *joie de vivre* – the kind of happiness Jayne MacDonald had that evening before strolling out when the portcullis came down to close the bar at 10.30 p.m.

The youngsters she was with had all drunk their fill of beer and they were hungry for fish and chips. The young man with Jayne talked about that night – Mark Hones of Rigton Approach, Leeds – said:

We danced at the Hofbrauhaus and about 10.30 we walked into the city centre with a number of friends. As we were walking she said she would like some chips in the centre, so we had some chips and then she said she had missed her last bus, so we sat on a bench by C & A. It got to about 12 o'clock and we went towards York Road by the Woodpecker. I told her I lived near there and my sister would drive her home, but she didn't seem bothered either way.

We got near the house and I saw that my sister's car wasn't parked there, so we walked up towards St James's Hospital. We went into a field and lay there for about three-quarters of an hour. I didn't try to have sex with her. Then we walked towards Beckett Street. I told her it was getting late and I would have to go home. I told her which way she could get home and the last time I saw her was by the main gates of St James's. We arranged to meet the following Wednesday.

Jayne went past the Florence Nightingale pub towards the taxi rank near the Dock Green pub, on the junction of Beckett Street and Harehills Road. There was no taxi available so she made her way towards Roundhay Road, where she often took the short cut from the supermarket where she worked. She was seen near the toilets at the Dock Green at 1.40 a.m. and she was seen walking along Bayswater Mount at 1.45 a.m.

It was some time shortly after this that Jayne was spotted

by the Ripper, prowling in his old car in the area of Round-hay Road. He had driven up Roundhay Road to Round-hay Park where he had murdered Irene Richardson in February 1977 and just off Roundhay Road he had dumped Emily Jackson's body in Manor Street, in January 1976. It was only a few paces from there, in Barrack Street, that he had picked up Wilma McCann in October 1975. Had the Ripper seen her come out of the field with the boy and assumed she was a prostitute, or followed her by car as she took the short cut towards Francis Street and Cowper Street, *en route* to her home? Whatever the answer, her mother had been assured by her that she would never get into a car with a stranger, not after Wilma McCann's death. She would also have repelled any advances a man in a car made to her if he was kerb crawling. Did he there-fore get out and approach her on foot and in a friendly-seeming manner which allayed her suspicions? Did he quite simply out-run her, or come up silently from behind?

Whatever the approach the Ripper attacked Jayne MacDonald within yards of her front door, in a frenzied attack which must have killed her within seconds. Her body was dragged behind a high wooden fence which surrounds the adventure playground for children, between Reginald Terrace and Reginald Street.

At breakfast time on Sunday morning, as church bells rang out over Leeds summoning early worshippers of half a dozen different denominations, three children saw her fully clothed body in the playground. Like the three previous Chapeltown victims she had not been sexually assaulted. Her brown handbag was lying four paces away. Nothing was missing from the bag which still contained her money, make-up and the letter addressed to her sister in South Africa. The police found spots of blood on the pavement outside the entrance to the playground. Although the street lights of Reginald Street had gone off at 11.30 p.m. the Ripper must have risked being seen with the body of

Jayne MacDonald on the pavement, before he had dragged it inside the fence to finish his ghastly work out of sight and earshot beneath the tall trees and the children's swings.

Detective Chief Superintendent Jim Hobson identified Jayne from the contents of her handbag and the forensic experts scraped at the bloodspots as the outraged people of Chapeltown heard the news of another murder in their midst.

On the morning of 27 June, when the newspapers realized that the killer they called the Yorkshire Ripper had slaughtered an innocent girl who lived six doors away from Wilma McCann in the red light area of Chapeltown, the story became national news. The chief constable of Yorkshire decided to put his senior, most experienced detective, George Oldfield, in charge of the Ripper murder hunt. A mobile police post with a towering radio mast and humming generator was set up in Reginald Street. The street was cordoned off and detectives with clip boards knocked on every door. Ten miles away at Wakefield, the Yorkshire police headquarters was more quiet than normal, for it was West Yorkshire Police Day, an annual event to which George Oldfield decided not to go. A fast car took him from his office in Wakefield to the scene of the crime.

Mr Oldfield, married with three children, an ex-grammar school boy and ex-Royal Navy petty officer who had taken part in the D Day landings, had succeeded Mr Donald Craig as head of CID, West Yorkshire in 1973. Donald Craig had solved all the seventy-three murder inquiries he had led in the three years he was head of the department. Mr Oldfield had a reputation to live up to and he himself had led the investigation in 1974 into the M62 coach bomb blast which killed twelve passengers and resulted in Judith Theresa Ward being sentenced to life imprisonment.

When Mr Oldfield arrived in Chapeltown, the people were clamouring for justice and a return of capital punishment. Petitions were about to be organized throughout Leeds. But Mr Oldfield had expressed his views on this in an interview with Sergeant Barry Shaw, the community affairs officer at Wakefield who edited the police newspaper the *West Yorkshireman*. He said he would advocate capital punishment for terrorists who had a total disrespect for human life, and added:

But on the question of capital punishment for murder, the difficulty is that there are so many shades of grey. No two murders are the same and who is to draw the line between the gallows and reprieve? I certainly believe the prerogative of mercy, if it is ever reintroduced, should not rest with the Home Secretary. I suggest it could be a panel of judges who spend their lifetime practising at the Bar and have a wealth of experience in dealing with offenders.

At the scene of the crime Mr Oldfield met Professor David Gee, the pathologist who saw all the Yorkshire victims and whose expert opinion on every Ripper killing would be vital to him. He also met Mr Hobson and Mr Hoban in Leeds. Mr Hobson was later to succeed Detective Chief Superintendent Hoban as head of Leeds CID when Mr Hoban was appointed deputy to the assistant chief constable (crime) in West Yorkshire, George Oldfield.

At the adventure playground in Reginald Street, the detectives looked down at Jayne MacDonald's body, clad in the blue and white halter-neck sun top with bare midriff and gingham skirt. Her brown tights were in place. A massive search of the area for the weapons used drew a blank, as in the cases of McCann and Jackson. Once again the Ripper had left few clues and the detectives knew that any lead they would get would come from a member of the public who had seen or heard something.

In the ultra-modern police headquarters at Millgarth, Leeds, a murder room map was to be filled with sightings and descriptions of vehicles during the next days. Every person who had seen Jayne that night or any motor vehicle in the area was tagged and the Reginald Terrace area map filled with sightings between 1 a.m. and 4 a.m. on the Sunday morning. A 10-year-old schoolboy's collection of car numbers was studied by detectives and also the diary of a housewife in Chapeltown who had started taking car numbers after being pestered by a kerb crawler. A woman living in Reginald Terrace told the police interviewer that she had heard sounds of banging and scuffling about 2 a.m. on Sunday coming from the direction of the adventure playground and the voice of a man with a Scottish accent mouthing obscenities. A witness came forward to say Jayne was in Bayswater Mount at 1.45 a.m. which placed her in the Reginald Street area at about 2.15 a.m.

George Oldfield made a series of appeals to the public to help the police in this murder hunt. He asked:

Innocent women who may have been propositioned by a kerb crawler who could be the Ripper trying to pick up a prostitute must contact the police urgently. Because it may have been the only time they were ever propositioned in this way, the man's face, peering out of his car window, should be still clear in their minds. While there are a number of men who do this, particularly in the Chapeltown area of Leeds, we believe the man we want must have tried it more than once and been turned down. If such a woman is frightened of telling her husband she should contact the police and she will be dealt with in confidence. This killer will strike again and the public hold the key to the success or failure of the police inquiry.

The public have the power to decide what sort of society they want. If they want murder and violence they will keep quiet. If they want a law-abiding society in which their women folk can move freely without fear of attack from the likes of the individual we are hunting, then they must give us their help. It is the little bits of apparently insignificant information so far as the public is concerned which is the vital information we want. This man has got to be caught. He has got to be stopped for the public good and the good of himself. There is no doubt in my mind that he will strike again. The big questions are When, Where, and Who is going to be his next victim? We have a clear picture in our minds now of the type of man we are looking for, and obviously no woman is really safe until he is found. We believe he is probably being protected by someone because on several occasions he must have returned home with heavily bloodstained clothing.

Mr Chris Tipple, deputy director of education for Leeds, instructed the headmasters of four schools, Roundhay High, Stainbeck High, City of Leeds High and Primrose Hill, to warn young girls to be wary. 'The girls will already know about police warnings, but we would like them to be warned not to go out at night unless they really have to. If they have to go out then they should always make sure they are accompanied or in groups. It is just commonsense advice.'

In a reconstruction of the night of Jayne's murder and her last walk home, Mr Oldfield said:

There is a strong possibility that she was waylaid after she left the boy near the Florence Nightingale public house in Beckett Street, Leeds, opposite St James's Hospital, early on the Sunday morning. We know that there was an AA patrol van parked nearby with two patrolmen in it. We now know that it was her intention to get a taxi from the kiosk near the Dock Green public house. If she could not get a taxi she had intended to make her way to the junction which is near the supermarket where she worked and from there we believe she would have made her way by one of several possible routes across the New Leeds area to Reginald Street.

Later Mr Oldfield said:

From witnesses that have come forward it is quite clear that there was a lot of activity in the area between 2 a.m. and 3 a.m. on Sunday and we are looking for the five people seen in that area about 2.30 a.m. A coloured man and woman were seen talking to two white women in the Reginald Street area and a fifth person – a coloured man – was seen walking or running nearby. It is quite apparent to me that there are a lot of people living in this area who have not come forward and who may well have seen or heard something significant.

Evening Post reporter Chris Bye described the devastation of the MacDonald family following the murder. 'Upstairs, Jayne's other sisters, Janet, aged 19, and Debra, aged 15 and her brother Ian, aged 12, are still in bed after four sleepless nights. Their father, Mr Wilfred MacDonald, is shaking and fighting to hold back tears as his daughter Mrs Carol Skorpen, aged 33, tells of her flight to England. "I have hardly eaten since I heard the news and have been taking tranquillizers before I set off. Jayne used to write to me quite regularly. We are a very close family. I have been living in South Africa for the past thirteen years. I last saw Jayne ten years ago when she was six years old."

'In the living room, darkened by drawn curtains, Jayne's mother, Mrs Irene MacDonald interrupted the conversation to say:

'Jayne was a bridesmaid at Carol's wedding at St Clements. We have been out to see Carol in South Africa. Carol has been a great comfort to us all, coming back. She has done her sisters and brother a lot of good. A neighbour, Hyman Bransberg, who lives down the road has been to see us. He thought a lot about Jayne. He is in the army but was given compassionate leave because he is so upset by Jayne's death. Everybody is being so kind to us. We had a letter from a Roundhay man whose fifteen-year-old son was drowned in an accident last year and another from a Gott's Park woman who lost her child when he caught a virus. My husband has been off from British Rail, Leeds City Station, for five months with chronic bronchitis. He was well on his way to recovery when the loss of Jayne came as a real blow. I am sure Jayne would never have accepted a lift in a car.

'She once got into a car she thought was a taxi, although it had no sign on. The driver took her down the wrong roads and she asked what was wrong. He said he had lost the way and she would have to direct him to her home. She told me afterwards that she was never so relieved to get home. All the family have been frightened of this killer ever since Wilma McCann was murdered.'

Mr Charles Wickert, manager of Grandways supermarket where Jayne had worked in the shoe department since 27 September, 1976 said:

Jayne was an attractive and extremely popular member of the staff. All her colleagues are shattered by the news. One girl was so stunned she had to be sent home by car. Jayne was a good, working girl, who got on with the job, willing and always helpful.

Mr Jack Bransberg said:

On Saturday evening she called to see us. She said she was going to a disco in Roundhay Road after the Astoria ballroom. She didn't ring and didn't arrive home and we thought perhaps she had gone back to her friends' home forgetting to let us know. Jayne was a sensible girl who knew right from wrong.

On 4 July, 1977 pretty 22-year-old policewoman Susan Phillips was shadowed by detectives reconstructing the two-mile route from St James's Hospital to Chapeltown, wearing a skirt and jacket identical to that worn by Jayne. 'It is necessary to get the right response from the public,' she said. 'But if I had been on my own, I would have been frightened. I think anyone would have been if they were alone in this area.'

In the coming weeks and months, 152 women were arrested and reported for prostitution in the Chapeltown area and a further 68 were cautioned. On the murder hunt, 170 police officers interviewed the residents of 679 houses in 21 streets. A total of 3,780 statements were taken from 13,000 people interviewed. The MacDonald family who had applied to the council for a new home before the murder moved to Scott Hall Road. Mrs MacDonald said:

In a way, moving house has helped us. I couldn't stand even to pass Jayne's bedroom door at the other house. Little things bring back memories: seeing Jayne's Bay City Rollers gear when we were moving house; listening to the song 'Raindrops Keep Falling', the tune played by one of Jayne's wind-up dolls; and hearing her favourite tune 'The Flasher' on a neighbour's radio.

About her 15-year-old daughter, Debra, she said:

We like her to stay in the area where we can see her all the time. We don't let her go out at night – and she should be beginning to enjoy life at her age. We make life hell for her ... but there is always the feeling that whoever is responsible for what happened to Jayne lives locally. Going to the shops is a trial. People stop me and ask how I feel. I know they mean well, but it brings it all back. They say they understand how we feel. But no one can know unless it has happened to them.

Jayne MacDonald's funeral cortège made its way to Harehills cemetery in thick fog, the coffin covered with flowers. Neighbours stood, bareheaded, in respect and all the family attended except 12-year-old Ian who was thought to be too young. In the late summer of 1979 the grave was marked with a plot number: 1486. Mr and Mrs MacDonald were still too distressed to arrange for Jayne's headstone.

George Oldfield was not to know it at the time, but the Ripper was to strike eight more times during the next two years, killing six of the women and almost killing the other two. The biggest murder hunt for the mass murderer would make George Oldfield, aged 53, the best known detective in Britain, with a following in America and in Germany and France. The hunt and his determination to catch the Ripper would become an obsessional cat-and-mouse game.

*

Only five days after the police were staging the reenactment of the last walk of Jayne MacDonald in Leeds, on Monday, 4 July, the Ripper was back in Bradford looking for a new victim among the Saturday night dancers and drinkers of the Manningham area. He cruised around in his old car on 9 July, waiting for a lone, unsuspecting woman, like Tina Atkinson, his last Bradford victim. The witching hour for the Ripper is usually after midnight when the last clubs and discos have emptied.

Maureen Long, aged 42, had dressed carefully in a long black evening dress to spend the evening at Tiffany's club in Manningham Lane and have a few drinks in the Bali Hai discotheque. The club and disco were full of life and music on Saturday night and 1,000 people would go there for an evening's drinking and dancing. It was a warm night as Maureen, only 5 ft 1 in tall, swinging her imitation brown leather handbag, sauntered past the taxi queues down towards the centre of Bradford in the direction of Hustlergate. It was some time between 2.15 a.m. and 2.45 a.m. that the Ripper drew up in his car alongside Maureen and stopped her. She was not sure of the time and never would be sure because the Ripper made a murderous attack on her in Bowling Back Lane which resulted in hideous skull fractures, hypothermia and memory loss. The surgeons who performed the delicate neurosurgical operation on Maureen Long at Leeds Infirmary were worried that there would be brain damage as a result of the deep wound.

She had been bashed on the head and then dragged fifteen yards from where the attack occurred, the same pattern the Ripper usually followed: proposition a girl, take her in the car to a lonely spot, follow her out of the car, smash her on the head from behind, then drag her, unconscious, out of sight, away from the street lights, preferably into an open field, parking lot, playing field or recreation ground. But he must have been disturbed or distracted from the usual pattern of stabbing and Maureen Long had enormous reserves of strength. She lay unconscious for several hours until her feeble cries for help were heard.

Mr Oldfield was told by Professor Gee that Mrs Long's injuries were the same as those suffered by the other women he had examined. Mr Oldfield waited by Mrs Long's bedside and was amazed that she had lived through her ordeal because she had lain, unconscious, from around 3 a.m. until 8.45 a.m. on Sunday, 10 July, when two women passers-by heard her calling out.

'She was suffering from hypothermia when she was found,' said Mr Oldfield. 'Had it been a colder night there is every possibility that she would have died of it.' She was also, surprisingly, able to give the police far more information than they had hoped for – a description of the man and the car.

On 12 July, the police issued a description of a man and a car which left Mount Street and went into Bowling Back Lane, Bradford, at 3.15 on Sunday morning. A man described as having puffy cheeks and noticeably large hands, white, aged 36 or 37, 6 ft 1 in tall, well built, with collar-length wiry blond hair, thick eyebrows, and wearing a white shirt and dark clothing. He was driving a white Mark 2 Ford Cortina with a black roof.

The police again appealed to the public for help, and asked them to call the FREEPHONE 5050 number set up after the Jayne MacDonald murder in Leeds. They again warned women not to walk alone at night, but their warnings were often ignored.

A week after the attack on Mrs Long, detectives set up tables in Tiffany's and questioned people who had seen her drinking there. They also questioned everyone in the taxi queues and neighbours at two addresses Mrs Long was using: Birks Hall Lane, Bradford and Donald Street, Farsley, Leeds. On 23 July, the Home Secretary, Mr Merlyn Rees, made a special trip to Leeds to talk to detectives hunting the Ripper. He was asked how concerned he was at the Ripper being at large for so long. He replied: 'I am no more concerned than the chief constable. Often piecing evidence together, considering it and analysing it, does take time, unless someone is there with a camera when the murder is committed.'

The Home Secretary was given statistics on the Ripper hunt: 304 officers at work on the case; 343,000 man hours already worked; 175,000 people interviewed; 12,500 statements taken, 101,000 vehicles checked.

chapter seven

Manchester is a sprawling northern industrial city which supports a population of $2\frac{1}{4}$ million, many of whom work at the National Computer Centre, or in the mail order business or of course in the textile industry on which the city built its reputation in the nineteenth century when cotton was king. Vast suburbs, such as Salford – home of the artist Lowry and actor Albert Finney – were built to house the millworkers. But aside from these mean streets of back-to-back grimy housing, Manchester also has its green spots.

A half-hour bus ride out from Manchester's Piccadilly lies the city's great necropolis, Southern Cemetery: acre upon acre of clipped grass verges, raked gravel paths, and carefully regimented tombstones. Passengers staying on the white and orange corporation double deckers to the southern terminus usually do so for one of three purposes: to tend graves, to work on the allotments adjoining the cemetery, or to make love.

In the evenings the wrought iron gates of the burial ground close at eight but this causes little inconvenience to knowledgeable lovers, for a two-minute walk down the dual carriageway, a link road to the M62 and M63, brings them to an open area of tall scrub grass, shielded from the road by high hawthorn hedges. Apart from a florist's shop and a garage there are few visible signs of life beyond this waste land except for the distant rows of cabbage, green beans and potatoes, their attendant greenhouses reflecting the sunlight. Cemetery and scrubland alike are a prostitute's delight. For one thing, the girls joke cynically, 'it's dead quiet'.

On the morning of Monday, 10 October, 1977 police at nearby Chorlton-cum-Hardy received a telephone call from one of the Princess Road allotment holders to say that he had found a body, that of a naked woman, lying in the grass alongside the cemetery fence. The caller sounded sick and the policemen answering the call soon discovered why: the body had the most terrible injuries that most of them had ever seen. Her tattered clothing lay scattered around in the grass and a hundred and fifty yards away was her green imitation leather handbag.

Detective Chief Superintendent Jack Ridgeway, head of Manchester CID, and Detective Superintendent Grange Catlow, in charge of the city's Serious Crimes Squad, paused only to pick up the local Home Office pathologist Reuben Woodcock before speeding out to the murder site – for murder it most obviously was. As they gazed down at the human remains, a reluctant question entered the minds of all three men: had the notorious Yorkshire Ripper crossed the Pennines into Lancashire?

The woman bore no identifying documents. By lunch-time, police had issued a description of her auburn hair, clothing and handbag – and a brief account of the circum-stances in which she had been found was published by the *Manchester Evening News* in its first edition. In the early evening the police received a telephone call from a Mr Alan Royle of Lingbeck Crescent, Hulme, a suburb not far from the Southern Cemetery. He said that he thought the description might fit his wife who was missing from home – though he believed she had gone to visit relatives in Scotland.

Mr Royle was taken to Manchester CID headquarters bringing with him a snapshot of his smiling, long-haired wife – his common law wife, as he later admitted. Even Mr Ridgeway and Mr Catlow could not be sure, looking at the attractive face in the photograph, that this was the woman whose body they had viewed that morning. Besides the massive blackening and bruising of the face due to the murderer's attack, the corpse had been lying in the open for some time; putrefaction had set in. And there had been rats in the field . . .

'Can I see her?' asked Alan Royle nervously. Detective Chief Inspector Thomas Fletcher of the Fingerprint Bureau had a better, more compassionate idea. 'Better not,' he said. 'Is there anything at home that she touched recently? Something in glass or metal perhaps that will have her fingerprints?' Mr Royle remembered that his wife had poured a glass of lemonade during their last evening together, 1 October. The bottle was still in the kitchen of their flat. Mr Fletcher had already taken the fingerprints of the corpse and the perfect set of latent prints he found on the lemonade bottle matched them exactly: there was now no doubt of the corpse's identity.

For the next forty-eight hours Alan Royle sat in an interview room, helping the police not only build up a picture of his wife's background and habits but eliminate himself as suspect from their inquiries.

His wife's name, he told them, was Jean Jordan; she spoke with the accent of her native Motherwell, Scotland. She had always, it appeared, been a bit of a 'loner'. Alan, a fully qualified chef, had met her on his way back from work in 1972; Alan was just twenty-one at the time and he was both attracted to and sorry for the sad-looking waif he saw wandering aimlessly around the concourse of Manchester's Victoria Station. He had offered her a cigarette and a cup of tea, both of which she accepted gladly. Shyly and haltingly she had told him that she had run away from home and headed for the nearest big city outside Scotland but she had no relatives in Manchester and little money. She had nowhere to stay and she was afraid that the police would pick her up and send her back to Motherwell.

'I had a little place in Newall Green, in Wythenshawe, and I took her back there,' said Alan. 'We were very happy. Two years after we met, Jean had our son Alan, who was named after me. He's three now and we have another boy James, who is one. We moved to our present place a few weeks ago so as to have more room for the children.'

The early idyllic happiness of the couple had not lasted, however. 'We started to grow apart. She found friends – girl friends, I thought – and would go out in the evenings with them, leaving me to look after the kids. Sometimes I would go out for a couple of days with the lads and leave her to it.'

On occasions Jean had taken a bus to the motorway and then hitched home to Scotland, where Alan believed she stayed with relatives. 'She always turned up later,' he recalled. 'A week last Friday, on 1 October, I went out for a drink and when I came back she had gone. When she didn't come back on Saturday morning I wasn't too alarmed. I thought she'd taken one of her trips to Scotland again. I didn't think to tell the police because she'd done it so often before. It wasn't until I read the paper with the description of the handbag and clothes that I started to worry . . .'

Alan Royle's story rang essentially true to the ears of the detectives and the story of his movements on the night his wife disappeared fitted. What they did not tell him was that another telephone call had been received in answer to the newspaper description. A girl named Anna Holt, known by the police to be a prostitute, had visited police headquarters as a result. The snapshot of Jean Jordan, who had lived her home life as Jean Royle was shown to her.

Anna nodded. 'I know her,' she said. 'That's Scotch Jean. She's on the game – she worked the same patch as me.' Police officers explained how badly Jean had been battered but Anna said that she felt strong enough to view the body. Flinching, she looked quickly at the dead features. 'Yes,' she whispered. 'That's her all right.'

Over a cup of strong tea, Anna Holt told what she knew of Jean Royle's life of vice. She had been on the streets for perhaps a couple of years; sometimes, particularly in winter, they had taken clients back to a flat in the city centre which was owned by a mutual friend. In warmer weather they had sometimes used the Southern Cemetery area, like many of their 'colleagues'.

'But poor Jean was not really cut out for it,' said Anna Holt. 'She was guilty about her kids. Just recently she told me that she was going to give it all up, pack it all in, settle down to a decent home life again . . .' This, too, seemed to fit the pattern which detectives were already beginning to build up. They had spoken to the Royles' neighbours in Lingbeck Crescent, all of whom agreed that she was a 'quiet and timid girl', essentially shy. 'She was definitely not the sort of woman who would talk to strangers in the street,' said one. Police also uncovered a strange coincidence during their investigation – unconnected with Jean's killing but bizarre nonetheless. Some time before, the previous occupant of the Lingbeck Crescent flat, 23-year-old Amina Thorne, had also met a violent death. She had died after jumping from the cab of a moving lorry. 'There seems to be a double death jinx on the place now,' said a neighbour, Mrs Ruby Matthews. 'Amina had only lived here about six months before she was killed, and Mrs Royle only moved in a few weeks back.'

From the facts which had emerged so far, one thing seemed abundantly clear: Jean had not been seen between 1 October, when she vanished and 10 October, when her body was found. The state of her body seemed to indicate that she had died shortly after leaving home for the last time. Now it was up to the forensic evidence produced by pathologist Reuben Woodcock to indicate hard facts.

In all cases of suspicious death in Britain a post-mortem examination is performed by a pathologist appointed by the Home Office and authorized by the local coroner. The object is not only to establish cause of death, but also where and when the victim died; the series of tests, measurements and examinations in each case are vastly complex. The first job facing the pathologist is a thorough external examination of the body and an examination of wounds in relation to clothing. The importance of this is obvious. To give a simple example, if a naked body is found stabbed through the chest and its discarded clothing shows a corresponding stab wound, it becomes apparent that the clothing has been removed after the stabbing. But to take the example further, the bloodstaining on the clothing will also give fair indication as to whether or not the stabbing took place before or after death; a newly dead body, when stabbed does not gush blood and a body dead for some time, hardly bleeds at all.

Post-mortem lividity can also indicate to the examiner the

time at which a naked body was stripped; the pinky-purple stains are usually fixed after the first few hours and tight clothing – bra straps, belts, pantie elastic – will leave an outline of white marks on the skin, which remain after the the clothing has been removed.

The examiner measures and notes the outward appearance of wounds and bruises, and the body is photographed from all angles and usually x-rayed. Taken together, the data gained give a good indication of the direction and force of the blows. The hands are examined for defensive slash marks caused while warding off a knife attack, and fingernail scrapings are taken to determine whether or not the victim has scratched the attacker, among other things. In the case of a naked body, footprints as well as fingerprints are taken from the corpse, so that any marks of bare feet found near the scene can be identified or eliminated. In cases of sex attack, the smoother parts of the body, such as the breasts or back, are treated with a solution of benzolene, alcohol and hydrogen peroxide to show up any latent fingerprints the killer may have left. Swabs are taken from vagina, rectum and mouth for laboratory analysis.

The state of putrefaction of the body is carefully noted at this time. Putrefaction begins as soon as rigor mortis wears off, beginning at the abdomen and spreading outwards; the time taken by the process varies according to the whereabouts of the body and its physical state; generally speaking a body decomposes in air twice as quickly as in water, and eight times as rapidly as one buried in earth. A young fit woman like Jean Royle, however, would resist decay reasonably well; the temperature and weather conditions over the period also have to be taken into consideration.

Next comes the internal examination. First the scalp is peeled back and the vault of the skull removed, exposing the brain, which is first checked in position and then taken out for closer inspection. An incision is made down the length of the trunk, the sternum or breastbone chiselled up and after a few swift scalpel strokes the entire body organs can be lifted out of the body cavity.

Then begins a further series of complicated checks. Their nature is set out in the classic text book *Medical Jurisprudence and Forensic Toxicology* by the late Professor John Glaister, which for years has been the handbook of British pathologists. The checks must include: 'an examination of all the organs of all the cavities of the body, even though the apparent cause of death has been previously found in one of them, since evidence contributory to the cause of death may be found in one or more of the others . . . inadvertent omission of a complete examination may readily invalidate a report.'

Blood and urine samples are taken and, what is most important, the stomach contents are examined and sent for analysis. Obviously these can give the pathologist a clear picture of death time in relation to the last meal or drink taken by the deceased. Alcohol, for instance, is absorbed into the blood stream from the stomach over a measurable period of time and different foods are digested at different rates. Normally a meal leaves the stomach in about four hours, but a large meal may stay up to five and generally speaking the fattier the meal the longer it stays.

Small slivers from the various bruised areas are excised from the body as well as sections of wounded skin for examination by a forensic histologist – a specialist in human tissue. Much can be told from such samples about the time and nature of a wounding, as Jack Ridgeway was to be reminded when Reuben Woodcock made his report; for it told a more sinister story than even the already brutal details had suggested.

Approximately forty minutes after leaving home on the evening of Friday, 1 October, Jean Royle had died at the hands of her killer, on the spare ground near Southern

Cemetery. He had smashed her skull with eleven powerful blows to the top of the head with a 'heavy weapon with a rounded end' – blows which left the entire face and head blackened with bruising. She had died as a result of these injuries. She had also suffered eighteen wounds on the abdomen and chest and a further six to her right side. But, said Mr Woodcock, there was more to it than that.

Eight days after her killing – probably after darkness on the night of Saturday, 8 October – the murderer had furtively returned to the hedgerow in which the body had lain undiscovered. He had dragged the body into the open, ripped off the clothing and flung the tattered remnants around a wide area. He had then stood over the corpse and inflicted further wounds with a sharp knife; one slash extended from the left shoulder to the right knee, another had torn open the abdomen, exposing the entrails. The deepest wound was seven inches longer.

Detective Superintendent Jack Ridgeway's first press conference was cautious to say the least. Questioned as to whether or not the dead woman had been a prostitute, he said: 'There is nothing to suggest it. It could be that while she was walking some motorist stopped and offered her a lift and that she expected she might have been able to get a lift up to Scotland. She has hitch hiked on occasions before.'

Was this horrific killing the work of the Yorkshire Ripper? Again Mr Ridgeway chose to sit on the fence. 'There are several similarities between our case and theirs, but there are also noticeable dissimilarities.'

He said no signs of sexual assault had been found on the body, though forensic experts had told police that 'indications of a sex attack' could have dissipated in the days since her disappearance. With these short statements the press had to be satisfied for the moment.

But Manchester CID had already been in touch with the Ripper hunt headquarters in Yorkshire and detectives from Lancashire had crossed the Pennines for a briefing session. With them, they took news of what they hoped might be a promising clue.

Like many prostitutes – who presumably could afford much better articles if they wished – Jean Royle had carried a cheap, imitation leather handbag. The primary reason for this is that prostitutes are notoriously at risk from thieves – either their own clients or 'muggers' – and few girls would care to complain to the police about the loss of a purse containing immoral earnings.

In Jean Royle's case, however, her handbag had not been stolen, but simply tossed aside and among its contents police found a brand new, crisp £5 note, serial number AW 51121565. A check of northern England banks produced swift and encouraging results. The note was one of a large batch which had been issued by a bank at Shipley, just outside Bradford, on 27 September, only four days before the Manchester murder. The batch had been split up and paid out to various local factories and businesses in time to go into workers' wage packets on Thursday and Friday, 29 and 30 September.

Now the chances of a £5 note from a Shipley area workman's Thursday or Friday pay packet crossing the Pennines to Manchester in the normal course of commerce in such a short time seemed extremely remote. So did the possibility of Jean Royle having had more than one client during her forty minutes of life after leaving home on the fatal Saturday night. Therefore it seemed almost certain that the man who had given her the £5 note and so carelessly – or disdainfully – left it in her handbag for the police to find was also her killer, who surely must work in the Shipley area.

Thirty Manchester detectives accompanied Jack Ridgeway and Grange Catlow to Yorkshire, where they met thirty West Yorkshire policemen under their boss George Oldfield. A disused schoolroom at Baildon, an outlying district of Shipley, was set up as a special incident room and the trans-Pennine team began their methodical investigations. By mid-October, Mr Ridgeway was still being cautious in his dealings with the press. He had released no details of the £5 note clue and would only say that detectives were interviewing workmen at firms in the Shipley, Bingley, and Bradford areas.

'At this stage we are not interviewing women, although we may do so at a later stage,' he said. And he was still uncommitted on the Ripper connection: 'As to whether there's a link with the unsolved murders in West Yorkshire, it is far too early to draw any conclusions.'

He did admit, however, that 'we are looking for a very strange man. I believe that the killer was annoyed or disappointed when Jean Royle's body wasn't found immediately. At some time, probably during the hours of darkness, he went back to the body to make sure that it was found.'

By mid-November, the bulk of the police inquiries at factories and workshops had been completed and at this point details of the note were issued to the general public. A list of every person, organization or firm to which the vital notes had been issued by the bank had been compiled and somewhere on the list, said Mr Ridgeway hopefully, was a clue which would lead them to the killer.

The hope was not to be realized. On 17 January, after three months and over five thousand interviews, the Baildon incident room was closed down, although a handful of detectives remained in the area, doggedly sifting and re-sifting the material which had been so painstakingly gathered.

There was further aggravation in store for the Manchester police later that year, this time from their colleagues in Yorkshire. At the inquests on the four Yorkshire prostitutes and that on Joan Harrison in Preston, few specific details of the injuries of the victims had been released. This was not simply censorship for the sake of protecting public sensibilities; the police were also nervous of 'imitation' killings if certain clues known only to them were released. These clues would, it was hoped, identify the killer uniquely at a later date.

But on 31 May, 1978, at Jean's inquest, Reuben Woodcock described in great detail the wounds he had found on Mrs Royle's body and the coroner, Mr Roderick Davies, said that it was a 'revolting case in which the killer had ripped up the victim's stomach'. He added – not entirely accurately as far as the time sequence was concerned: 'We can assume she was knocked unconscious and then whoever committed this appalling crime ripped her up.' For the first time the jury was told that the killer was 'believed to be the Yorkshire Ripper'. A statement was read from Anna Holt, the prostitute who had identified the body, about Jean Royle's vice activities and the jury returned a verdict that she had died of multiple head injuries, 'unlawfully killed by a person or persons unknown'.

The wounds on Jean Royle's body were by no means identical to those of the other victims – a fact which had caused much of Jack Ridgeway's reticence to ascribe the killings to the Ripper in the first place; and in fact Reuben Woodcock and Coroner Davies were sticking to the letter of the law in revealing what they did. Since the time of Edward I, English Common Law has required that 'all the injuries of the body, also the wounds, ought to be viewed; and the length, breadth, and deepness, with what weapon, and in what part of the body the wound or hurt is . . . all things must be enrolled in the roll of the coroner.'

Nevertheless, senior West Yorkshire policemen were annoyed that so much had been revealed. Most of them must have read the facts of the original Jack the Ripper case of 1888, and been aware of an almost parallel wrangle which went on following the inquest on Marie Kelly, the prototype Ripper's final victim. In that case, Coroner Roderick MacDonald, himself a police surgeon, had bluntly

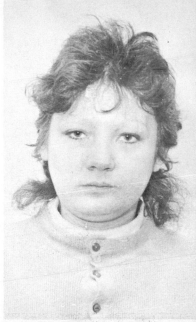

above Wilma McCann, aged 28.
Murdered in Leeds, October 1975

above right Joan Harrison, aged 26.
Murdered in Preston, November 1975

right Emily Jackson, aged 42.
Murdered in Leeds, January 1976

above left Irene Richardson, aged 28.
Murdered in Leeds, February 1977

above Patricia Atkinson, aged 33.
Murdered in Bradford, April 1977

left Jayne MacDonald, aged 16.
Murdered in Leeds, June 1977

above right Jean Royle, aged 20.
Murdered in Manchester.
October 1977

right Helen Rytka, aged 18.
Murdered in Huddersfield,
January 1978

above far right Yvonne Pearson, aged 22.
Murdered in Bradford, January 1978

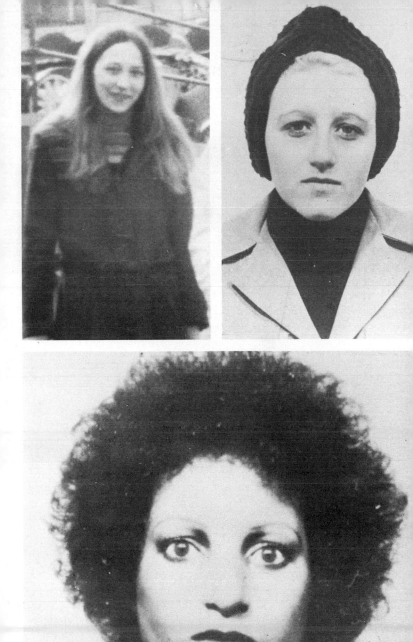

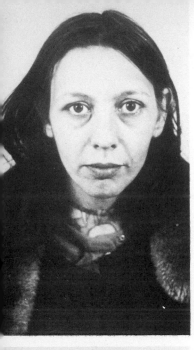

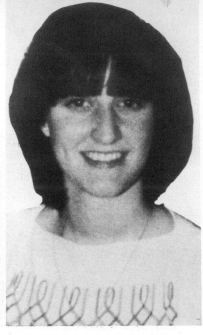

above left Vera Millward, aged 40.
Murdered in Manchester, May 1978

above Josephine Whitaker, aged 19.
Murdered in Halifax, April 1979

left Barbara Leach, aged 20.
Murdered in Bradford, September 1979

The scene after Wilma McCann's body was found
Police photograph of the Yorkshire Ripper's letter
Assistant Chief Constable George Oldfield

Dear Officer,
                                        March 23rd 79
        Sorry I haven't written, about a year to be
exault, but I haven't been up North for quite a while.
I wasn't kidding last time I wrote

                                                    That
was last month, so I don't know when I will
get back on the job but I know it wont be
Chapeltown too bloody but there maybe
Bradford, Manningham. Might write again
if up North.
                    Jack the Ripper
PS Did you get letter I sent to Daily Mirror
in Manchester.

An intensive police search for clues

Using police dogs to cover the surrounding area for clues

George Oldfield listening to the tape recording made by the man claiming to be the Yorkshire Ripper

Manning the public response to hearing the Ripper tape

WEST YORKSHIRE METROPOLITAN POLICE

MURDER

OF

JAYNE MICHELLE McDONALD,
16 years, at Leeds, Sunday, 26th June, 1977

Did you see her after 10 p.m. Saturday, 25th June?

Do you know her?

CAN YOU HELP?

IF SO, PLEASE CONTACT THE POLICE. ALL INFORMATION WILL BE TREATED CONFIDENTIALLY. TELEPHONE LEEDS 454173, 454197 OR INFORM ANY POLICE OFFICER

One of the police posters appealing for information on the murders stated: 'There is other evidence which I do not propose to call, for if we at once make public every fact brought forward in connection with this terrible murder the ends of justice might be retarded.'

It was almost certainly this lack of specific evidence which had given rise, in the case of the Yorkshire Ripper, to curious and widespread rumours: that he had pulled out his victims' entrails, placed tin cans and beer bottles, money, or even a football in their wounds, cut off their nipples and so on. Whether or not such ill-founded speculation could be of either help or hindrance to the police in their inquiries, only they could decide. In any case, by the time of the Royle inquest on 31 May, 1978 Yorkshire police were busy with two further Ripper murders, while Jack Ridgeway himself was working night and day on the death of Vera Millward, the Ripper's second Manchester victim, which had occurred on 18 May.

For Alan Royle and his two motherless children, the heartbreak was only just beginning, however. An interview in the *Manchester Evening News* on 3 April, 1979 told the whole sad story. Shattered by the tragedy he had been unable to concentrate on work and had lost his well-paid job as a chef. Instead, he had taken an unskilled labouring job at an engineering factory, coming home in the evenings to tend his infant son Alan, who had been retarded by his mother's death although he had previously been a bright child. At four and a half years old Alan could speak only a few monosyllabic words. In the summer of 1978 things seemed to take a turn for the better when Alan met and married his wife Sylvia after a five-day whirlwind courtship. At first they had rented accommodation, but had later moved to Sylvia's mother's for the winter.

'Sylvia was great with the kids and they both loved her,' he said. 'She was so understanding about Jean. She used to sit and make me talk about it so I could get it out of my system. She was not jealous – she used to buy flowers and make me take them down to the grave.' But again the idyll did not last. Sylvia Royle became depressed when she learned that she was pregnant and further that the couple's only chance of a council house was to move into a 'homeless unit' – a hostel at Altrincham, Cheshire. They moved, but Sylvia's depression deepened until one night Alan Royle returned home to find – with a heart-stopping sense of *déjà vu* – that she had left him and gone back to her mother.

'If only I could get a house away from all the memories, perhaps Sylvia would come back and we could start a new life and put everything behind us,' he said. 'Even memories of Jean.'

chapter eight

Huddersfield is not always a miserable place. When the sun shines there is a cheerful brightness about the newly cleaned civic buildings and a highlight on the smile of the face of the great stone lion which crouches above St George's Square. There is a buoyant sweep to the line of the six-lane elevated highway carrying traffic westwards along the M62 and the Monday market, with its Punjabi and Urdu tradesmen, is a kaleidoscope of colour. In the distance the blue-green mound of Almondbury, man-made over 4,000 years ago, dominates the skyline, topped by a monumental tower raised to Queen Victoria when Huddersfield was at its peak as a woollen town.

Sadly, Huddersfield is not noted for sunshine. Mist rolls down from its hills in early autumn, only to be replaced by melancholy drizzle and, later, freezing sleet. The subdued rumble of lorries on the motorway mingles with the mournful lowing of beasts waiting for death in the town abattoir next to the market place; from the railway viaduct arches of Great Northern Street, water drips steadily into the darkness below. The joyous voices of the world famous Huddersfield Choral Society, raised in their twice-yearly renderings of Handel's 'Messiah', cannot quite obliterate the echo of that dripping water and the furtive sounds which accompany it. Roman whores plied their trade under viaduct arches – *fornix* – giving the English language the word 'fornicate'. At least the prostitutes and male homosexuals of Great Northern Street have tradition at their backs...

Tuesday, 31 January, 1978 could hardly be said to have dawned at all. The sky gradually turned a lighter shade of grey, from which big feathery flakes of snow fell on to the waking town. It was cold, but not too cold for the snow to settle and as the day wore on the streets became treacherous with yellow slush. Up on Highfields Hill, twin sisters Elena and Rita Rytka lay huddled together in their chilly nest, drowsing the day away.

The twins were born within minutes of each other on 3 March, 1959 and had been inseparable since then despite the most monstrous odds. They had stayed together as small children when their Italian mother had broken with their Jamaican father, they had clung to each other through various Roman Catholic hostels and schools and had even managed the almost impossible feat – largely through their own efforts – of finding foster parents with sufficient money to keep them together in their early teens. But in the past few weeks, life had seen them at their lowest ebb; Helen – as Elena preferred to be called – had become a prostitute, walking the streets of Huddersfield. Now on this winter's day her existence was drawing to a close.

'Enderley' had once been a proudly detached Victorian villa in a series of several lining Elmwood Avenue, standing well above the smoky industrial town centre. Now the name endured only as a fading inscription on the crumbling stonework. The house itself had become 'thirty-one' and the former downstairs drawing room which was the Rytka twins' home was described as 'flat three' – an appellation which was, in the circumstances, ridiculously grand.

Flat three cost the girls £5 per week and was a room opening on to a draughty, stone-flagged passageway, down which was their shared lavatory. Rita, a former art student, had done her best with the place after moving in during the previous November. She had whitewashed the walls and scraped up enough money to buy matching curtains and carpet, brilliant in orange and brown and red. But the cold and the all-pervading damp had begun to erode her work; whitewash flakes sprinkled the new carpet like dandruff, and the paper which covered the ceiling hung in moist bubbles.

Their double bed with its light blue counterpane took up the whole of one wall, while the rest of the sparse furniture consisted of a table, chairs, and a wardrobe. Scattered around were the sisters' cheap but trendy clothes. It was a poor hole for human beings to live in, but for the Rytka twins it was the only home they had ever had to themselves.

Bernardina, their mother, had been born in Venice and was herself the product of a broken home. Her father died when she was small and she spent seven years in a foster home until, in 1953, she moved to England 'to seek a better life'.

After a spell in London she moved north to Leeds and met her first husband, a Jamaican named Eric Rytka. The couple, both immigrants, found it hard to make ends meet and at four months old Helen and Rita were placed in council care. Despite the birth of a further set of twins, Anthony and Angela, the Rytka fortunes improved sufficiently for Helen and Rita to be able to move back home with their parents shortly before their fifth birthday.

Home was a ramshackle terraced house in Leopold Street, Chapeltown, but at least the family were together and happy for a while. They were staunch Catholics and attended Mass together every Sunday morning at the Church of the Holy Rosary, the white gloves of the girls standing out against their coffee-coloured skin. At five they became eligible for school and attended the St Charles Roman Catholic Junior School, Burmantofts, not far from their Leeds home, where their head teacher Sister Joseph later remembered them as 'bright children, talented musically and artistically and good all-round scholars. And they were essentially loving children,' she said. 'They were held back only by their difficult home background.'

In fact the brief spell of happiness enjoyed by the Rytka family began to evaporate over the next few years. Eric and Bernardina split up and were finally divorced. In 1969, when Helen and Rita were ten, the Leeds Social Services Department took responsibility for them and, as Roman Catholics, responsibility for them passed to the Leeds Diocesan Rescue, Protection, and Child Welfare Society, which found them places at St Theresa's Home, a hostel run by the Sisters of the Holy Family of Bordeaux at Thistle Hill, Knaresborough.

Knaresborough, a small country town about fifteen miles from Leeds, was a far cry from the Chapeltown slums and at first its beauty and curious history acted as a stimulus to the twins' lively young minds. But the beauty of the countryside and the kindness of the nuns could not obliterate the fact that St Theresa's was an institution. As a year went by, then two, Helen and Rita began to pine for the home life they had known so briefly. Sometimes, they knew, children from St Theresa's found foster parents, but they were also painfully aware that they had pitifully little to recommend them. They were not bonny babies any more, but gawky teenagers, angular and awkward and showing nothing of the beauties they were to become. They refused to be separated, which meant that anyone adopting them would have double the expense. And, of course, they were 'coloured'. There seemed to be little hope.

Then, in 1974, the sisters read a series of articles in the *Evening Post* which boosted their spirits. On 6 May, they sat down and wrote a letter to the paper, which was published the same week.

Dear Sir/Madam, I am writing to you sending my views on fostering and adoption. I have read two of your articles on fostering and I think it is a marvellous idea. I am a child in care and have been for twelve years. If my twin sister and I got fostered out together it would be like winning £1,000 on the football pools. But money is not involved. LOVE is. . .
To get fostered out together means to us a place of love and care and it is then that you feel wanted, because someone somewhere realizes what love really is and to get fostered out is part of love itself. We can only wait, hope and pray to get fostered out together, but some day I hope we will.

Their joint prayers were answered within days of publication. A Dewsbury civil servant and his childless wife, who remained anonymous during the publicity of later years, read the letter and poem. A few weeks later the twins were installed in the square-built stone house set in a large garden which was to be their home for the next two years. Their foster parents were everything they had hoped for; though Catholic, they were fairly liberal in their views and saw the need for the girls to develop along the lines of their natural talents. And the house was big enough to provide them with separate bedrooms – the first time Helen and Rita had known such luxury.

For the remaining years of their education the pair attended the St John Fisher Roman Catholic High School in Dewsbury, where Rita concentrated on drawing and painting: her ambition had become fixed on a course at nearby Batley Art School. Helen, on the other hand, was like an uncaged bird, revelling in the freedom from institutionalized life; though talented, she allowed her academic studies to slide in favour of dancing and singing. At 16, both she and her sister had classically beautiful faces and lissom figures and almost every evening found Helen dancing at the Pentagon disco in Mirfield, not far from her home. At weekends the pair would travel further afield; their twin siblings Anthony and Angela were living in a flat together in Laisterdyke, a suburb of Bradford and they either went there or to the Merrion Centre in Leeds. Helen, open and forgiving, visited her mother Bernardina at her home in Victoria Terrace, Leeds.

In the summer of 1976, the Rytka sisters' school days came to an end. Rita's hard work had won her a grant to Batley Art School, whilst Helen's love of dancing had damaged her chances of high examination marks. She felt, with her inside knowledge of children's homes, that one day she might become a children's nurse, able to give a little of the sympathy and warmth which she herself had missed. In her daydreams she also saw herself as a pop singer, making a fortune, travelling the world. In the meantime she took a £20 per week job as a packer at Bysel sweets factory in Heckmondwike. She was young, after all. She had all the time in the world . . .

In September, 1976 the Rytka twins left their foster home in Dewsbury to move in with Tony and Angela at the tower block flat they occupied in Laisterdyke. The move was handy for both sisters: Helen travelled about seven miles to work by bus, while Rita had a further mile to go to college.

Helen enjoyed life at Bysel sweets factory, a friendly company which employed about forty girls and a handful of men. A manageress at the firm later recalled her with affection:

She was a lovely girl with a smashing figure, though she caused no jealousy. She could easily have got big headed with her looks, but she wasn't pushy or forward – she rarely bothered much with men, though she was friendly with them. She was a good hard worker, quietly cheerful, but the most fantastic thing about her was her timekeeping. She was never late. Even in the hard winter around Christmas of 1977, when the buses were snowed up and some services were stopped, she managed to get here – and on time too. She told me once that rather than go home to Bradford she had caught a bus as far as it went into Batley and then walked through the snowdrifts to her old foster home in Dewsbury. The following morning she did the journey in reverse. She was very conscientious.

In the autumn of 1977, Rita Rytka left the flat in Laister-dyke and for the first time in her life went to live alone in the Highfields room in Huddersfield – at the same time dropping out of her Batley Art School course. She had become more withdrawn and introverted, while her sister, with her regular weekly wage packet, was out dancing almost every night.

But Helen missed her. At Christmas she visited their mother in Leeds, looking for Rita. Mrs Rytka recalled: 'Her one worry was for Rita. She kept asking me if I had any idea where she was; she hadn't heard from her since she left Tony and Angela's, but I couldn't tell her because I didn't know where she was either.'

Somehow, the twins met up and shortly after Christmas Helen moved into the damp room in 'Enderley'. Two weeks later, in mid-January, Helen gave up her job at Bysel. 'It came as a complete surprise,' said her colleague. 'She gave no reason. She just said that she was leaving to go and live with her sister in Huddersfield, said goodbye to everybody, picked up her money and that was the last we saw of her.'

The truth was that at some time after their reunion, Helen had decided to sell herself as a prostitute and

Huddersfield was a good place in which to operate. The town which had been the birthplace of such establishment figures as Sir Harold Wilson, former Prime Minister, and film star James Mason had developed a thriving red light area with its centre in the Great Northern Street area, just off the market place; the railway arches of the viaduct were its 'brothels'.

But sex under the arches was the domain of the lower end of the Huddersfield vice market and there is no evidence that Helen Rytka had sunk to this level. She was eye-catchingly attractive, particularly so under street lamps, and was easily able to operate the 'car trade', being picked up by clients in Great Northern Street, Alder Street, or Hillhouse Lane and driven to secluded spots for sex on the outskirts of the town.

As the sky darkened on that last late Tuesday afternoon, 31 January, 1978, Helen and Rita rose shivering to plug in their electric kettle for tea. Helen dressed quickly in black lace underwear, black corduroy jeans and black polo-neck sweater before fluffing out her Afro hairstyle and skilfully applying touches of make-up around her eyes and mouth. By 8.30 p.m. the winter's night had long closed in completely, but the sodium lights of the town centre were reflected in the powdery snow which was still drifting down, muffling the noise of the lorries on the motorway flyover below the girls' window.

Rita, too, was dressed and Helen finally donned a short imitation brown fur jacket against the cold and followed her out along the draughty passage, closing the half-hung hardwood door behind her at the far end before stepping out into the night.

A steep pathway worn into the grass of the hillside led them down, in single file, to the market area. At about 9 o'clock Mrs Gwen Smith, wife of the market supervisor Fred Smith, and their son Paul were walking home from Huddersfield Sports Centre; the Smiths occupied one of the few houses in Great Northern Street. They later remembered seeing the girls patrolling slowly, Helen on one side of the street, Rita keeping pace on the other.

The two were not without caution; their usual arrangement was that if Helen was picked up in a car she would return to Great Northern Street and meet up with Rita before taking her next client. On this evening something went wrong with the system.

At about 9.10 p.m., a dark-coloured car drew up alongside Helen. From across the street and in the distortion caused by the street lighting, Rita could not make out whether its colour was black or dark blue, but it was a Ford, either a Consul or Granada. As the door opened and the interior light went on, Rita saw that the driver was a thinly built individual in his late 30s or early 40s, his dark brown hair cut with a fringe and short sideboards. Then the door closed and the car drove off.

Shortly afterwards, Rita was picked up in a Datsun and when the driver returned her to the meeting point some time later there was no sign of her sister. The night was cold, and traffic was sparse. After waiting a while longer, she made her way back up the steep path to Highfields.

The following morning produced no sign of Helen and by now Rita was thoroughly frightened. It was very unlikely that Helen would agree to spend the night with a client. Something must have happened to her. On the other hand Rita was naturally hesitant about going to the police and telling them everything that had occurred; but the ties which had bound her to Helen for so long were very strong. She made her way down to the Huddersfield Police Station and reported her sister as 'missing'.

The daytime business of Great Northern Street is centred on a timber yard which straggles alongside and under the railway viaduct and which was unfenced at the time of Helen's disappearance, where it abutted on to the roadway. Apart from the opportunities it offered the area's prostitutes – the piles of wood and the numerous lock-up huts formed many secluded nooks – it had long been a source of minor irritation to Huddersfield police because of the invitation it offered to thieves and to drunken 'dossers' who slept, lit dangerous fires and sometimes fought each other among the timber stacks.

As one timber-yard worker commented: 'All sorts of things happen around here at night. It doesn't bother us any more, the things we find. We take them in our stride.'

On the morning of Wednesday, 1 February, a truck driver pulled his laden wagon to a stop in the yard, stepped down from his cab and immediately spotted a pair of black lace panties. The yard foreman was amused; he told the driver, as he signed the delivery note, that they had found bloodstains near one of the huts. It must have been a 'fair old night'. Later, he told a local reporter, they had 'hung the knickers up on a nail for t'lads to laugh at'.

Meanwhile, police inquiries were proceeding along the normal lines for 'missing persons'. Tony and Angela Rytka were visited at their Laisterdyke flat, but had seen no sign of Helen. Bernardina Rytka told officers of her daughter's last visit during Christmas week and at the girl's former foster home in Dewsbury the civil servant and his wife expressed concern to the police officer who called them; they had not seen Helen for some weeks.

At first Rita had told the police as little as possible, but as their inquiries proved fruitless she confessed to them that Helen had been working as a prostitute; she spoke of the car Helen had entered and told about the arrangement to meet back in Great Northern Street. The head of Huddersfield CID, Detective Chief Inspector John Stainthorpe, suspected the worst the moment he heard the news. He ordered an immediate search of the timber yard in Great Northern Street and at ten minutes past three on the afternoon of Friday, 3 February – ten minutes after the search began – Helen's body was found.

The corpse lay beneath one of the railway arches at a secluded corner of the yard, hedged in on two sides by buildings; it was screened from the rest of the premises by a pile of timber baulks. It was completely naked in the melting snow and bore all the grisly trademarks of the Ripper – head shattered from multiple blows, the bare torso punctured by numerous wounds.

Mr Stainthorpe contacted CID headquarters at Wakefield and arranged for Professor Gee to be brought to the site. Detective Chief Inspector Bill Little, a coordinating officer from Wakefield, had set up an 'incident room' in a cramped and claustrophobic corner of Huddersfield's Castlegate police station by the end of the afternoon. Each of Mr Little's handpicked team had a specific duty – card-indexing vehicles reported, checking with the area Criminal Records Office on persons interviewed, marking up maps and charts and so on, as well as manning the three telephones. All days off and annual leave were cancelled and the full team worked from 9.30 in the morning until 9.30 at night, with a skeleton staff on duty during the other hours. A police press officer explained:

Any and every piece of information is fed into the system, either from our men or from the public and all action to be taken is coordinated from here. The detectives working in the field – the men 'on the ground' – each have a team leader, who takes his instructions from here. All the previous information on the Ripper's activities is within easy access of the incident room and our files are constantly updated.

As darkness fell, the murder site took on the eerie unreality of a film set. The snow had turned to bitter drizzle, falling through the beams of the blazing arc lights, which drained faces of colour and cast sharp-edged shadows to the rear of the yard. The high railway arches amplified and distorted the throb of the big diesel generators and dwarfed even the uniformed policemen in their tall helmets and waterproof capes.

Watching the activity from her door in Great Northern Street was Mrs Ethel Cowan. She told reporters:

Prostitutes have been using this area ever since I moved in thirteen years ago and we are always bothered by the noise of cars and their doors slamming late at night. My husband Alfred and I know what's going on and there have been some complaints, but the nuisance hasn't been stopped. And now this murder has really shocked us both. I shan't go out on my own at night now. It's too dark and lonely a place for that.

The following morning, Saturday, George Oldfield made a short statement to the press, briefly describing Helen's wounds and the car into which she had climbed while watched by her sister. Cautious as ever, he ended: 'As the indications are at present, I cannot discount the possibility that the man we are looking for is the man responsible for similar attacks on women in West Yorkshire over the past two and a half years.'

The inquiry followed the usual, footslogging route; for the detectives and uniformed men there were no short cuts. The incident room telephones were ringing once every minute during the first few days and as each piece of information was logged it was passed on to the 'men on the ground' for following up. A patrol car took one man around the second-hand car dealers and car parks of the area in an effort to spot a suspicious white vehicle which he had seen on the night of Helen's death. The car was traced and eliminated. Several men were interviewed after being reported 'loitering' in the area; three were held for several hours at Leeds Town Hall's old 'Bridewell' cells before being released. One man the police wished to interview was given what amounted to an amnesty by George Oldfield. He had been seen lurking near a public lavatory. Mr Oldfield said: 'I don't care what he was doing there.

He may have been a homosexual, he may have been stealing wood – I'm not interested, as long as we can find him and he can tell us what he saw.'

On 7 February, at 3 o'clock in the afternoon, the FREE-PHONE line was brought into operation. By ringing the Freephone 5050 number, callers were put directly through to the Millgarth police headquarters; soon the number was ringing incessantly.

In the week following the murder, further snow fell on Huddersfield, muffling traffic noise and thinning out the numbers of people on the streets. As darkness fell each night, a small army of police officers, men and women working in pairs, descended on the red light area. Most were in plain clothes and all kept a 'low profile' according to their instructions. A handful of girls hung about in bars, cafés, and on street corners – though always under bright street lights. The face of Helen on the police poster stared down from grimy windows and sooty brick walls. The few girls who had known Helen spoke of her as 'friendly' and 'likeable'. One woman, a nurse, recalled: 'I knew her by sight and would sometimes exchange greetings with her as I came home from netball matches. She'd say hello and ask how the match went. I last saw her just before Christmas. She was really friendly.'

On the morning of 9 February, George Oldfield appeared on the highly popular Jimmy Young Radio Show. In an appeal to housewives, he pointed out that someone – perhaps a wife, mother or girl-friend of the man – probably knew the Ripper's identity. He begged them to come forward if they knew anything at all, or suspected anything, in order to help prevent a further murder.

Meanwhile in Huddersfield another appeal was being made, this time to the immigrant community. Two posters were commissioned, one in Urdu and one in Punjabi, from leading members of both communities. Two hundred were circulated in Huddersfield, and others posted in Bradford.

The community relations officer responsible explained:

The Punjabi is one headed 'Sympathetic Murder'. To Asians from the Punjab, a sympathetic murder is one in which an innocent victim is killed, thus attracting the sympathy of the public. It usually means a brutal and savage attack and we believe that in this case it is more likely to bring information from the immigrant community in the town.

But since the death of Wilma McCann many highly publicized appeals had already been made by the police and apart from a mass of valuable information no major clue to the killer's whereabouts had been forthcoming. If someone did know where he was, or suspect his identity, perhaps an offer of hard cash might produce results?

So, in any case, reasoned the *Yorkshire Post*, the country's old-established, influential and highly respected morning paper. The idea of a reward ran counter to official Home Office policy, but the newspaper had a tradition of taking unpopular, though necessary, stands. In 1939, for instance, it had vigorously opposed the appeasement policy of Neville Chamberlain and the Conservative Party, despite its own true blue history – and its stand had been proved right.

The Home Office announced that it 'did not regard rewards as effective measures', largely because they set a precedent – there was always a danger that in future the public would hang back until the reward was large enough before giving information. The *Yorkshire Post* and its sister paper the *Evening Post* disagreed and announced the offer of £5,000.

Most police officers privately agreed that a reward would probably be helpful and so did the general public. Hard on the heels of the newspaper announcement, two public funds were established to raise extra money. Five Yorkshire businessmen agreed to put up £1,000 each, while six Leeds councillors formed a committee to raise further cash, collecting in bars, works canteens, churches and other public meeting places. But Chief Constable Ronald Gregory disagreed with public fund raising, if only on the grounds that the money would be hard to return if the Ripper were caught by police action alone. The flow of money slowed after his remarks were published, and eventually £1,000, collected anonymously in boxes, was given to charity, while the businessmen received their cheques back.

Nevertheless, the action provoked a response from the County Council's Police Committee, which put up £10,000 to join the *Yorkshire Post* reward; in November of 1978 the committee approved 'without discussion' the doubling of the reward, bringing the total to £25,000. A poster showing pictures of the victims and announcing the reward said:

How to claim that cash. If you wish to remain anonymous – for the present – give a personal code word and a six-figure number. This will be your own identification code. If your information leads to the conviction of the Ripper you will be able to claim your reward by identifying yourself with the personal code word and number. As an additional safeguard you should tear off and keep a corner of the paper on which the letter to Mr George Oldfield is written.

Since the discovery of her sister's body, Rita Rytka had been staying at a secret address in Bradford, guarded night and day by a police officer. Police reports stated that she was 'bearing up well' under the considerable strain and on 13 February, ten days later, she emerged to meet the press for the first time.

Escorted by her solicitor, and with a dark-haired woman friend who refused to identify herself, Rita walked into the conference room. She looked frail and was dressed in her habitual blue jeans, with a striped sweater, a silver torque around her neck and a belt with a big, square 'Winchester rifle' buckle. In one hand she clutched a handkerchief, tightly balled; in the other a statement written by herself on a page torn from an exercise book. She managed a slight smile for photographers and then began to read in a clear, small, halting voice:

Helen was a very happy girl and her main ambition in life was to sing. The circumstances did not allow her to fulfil that ambition. She was very close to me. No loss could be greater than of her. I hope the public will not forget her. I am helping the police all I can and I hope anyone who has information will show sympathy and come forward.

Friday, 3 March, 1978 was Rita Rytka's nineteenth birthday. Throughout the years, in homes and institutions, she and Helen had managed to celebrate their day together somehow: sometimes with a small iced cake, sometimes by drawing each other birthday cards. On this damp Friday there was no celebration; Rita spent the day sitting at the window of her brother's tower block flat, gazing out over the shining roofs of Laisterdyke. A policeman and woman sat near her. They knew that the forthcoming week held two ordeals for her.

The first came on Monday morning, when Kirklees coroner Mr Philip Gill opened and adjourned the inquest on Helen, leaving the matter in abeyance for the statutory year. The whole proceedings were quiet and subdued. Rita took the stand and told her brief tale:

My sister was born in Leeds and was an unemployed confectionery assistant. I last saw her on the evening of Tuesday, January 31, in Great Northern Street, Huddersfield, and at that time she was getting into a car at about 9.10 p.m. Later I became concerned because she hadn't returned home and early the following morning I went and made inquiries of the police. I heard and saw nothing more of her until her body was found on Friday, 3 February.

Before adjourning, Coroner Gill appealed for anyone knowing the whereabouts of the killer to come forward. After glancing distastefully at the pathologist's report, he laid the paper aside and told the court:

Helen was attacked with the utmost callousness and brutality. If the full details could be revealed they would shock even our modern brutal society. I can well understand that if a person is a relative or close friend they might have some mental anguish or reservations about coming forward, but unless this person is apprehended there is the greatest possible likelihood that he will commit another, similar offence and we shall have another death on our hands. The person who is feeling mental anguish will have the added, almost intolerable burden of another death, which they could possibly have avoided. Their anguish – and their responsibility – will be even greater than it is now.

Rita Rytka's second ordeal of that week came on Thursday, 9 March, when her sister was buried at Scholemoor Cemetery, Bradford. About thirty people turned up, including Rita, her mother, her brother and sister, several of Helen's former workmates, representatives of the staff and advisers of the Knaresborough home and a sprinkling of burly detectives. The burial was preceded by a half-hour service in St Anthony's Church, Clayton, Bradford, conducted by Canon John Murphy, who was administrator of the Leeds Catholic Rescue Society which had cared for the Rytka twins as children. His assistant was Father Michael Killen, the priest who had heard their first confessions at Knaresborough.

For the detectives at the cemetery there was little time to linger as the clay was heaped in on top of Helen Rytka's coffin. They had another problem on their hands: one which increased their apprehension as each day passed. A Bradford prostitute named Yvonne Pearson had been missing from home since Helen's disappearance and there was still no sign of her, despite a protracted and intensive hunt.

Meantime Leeds police were also busy after one of the strange coincidences which sometimes occur in crime had brought them racing to a house in Chapeltown once again. On Sunday, 20 February, 1978 police found another Mrs Richardson dead in the same house as that inhabited by the Ripper's fourth victim, Irene Richardson. The woman in the Cowper Street corner house was Mrs Winifred Maude Richardson, aged 47, and she was no relation to Irene Richardson. A West Indian, 40-year-old Charles Egbert 'The Colonel' Gardiner, was also dead with stab wounds, and a third person, Pauline Woofitt, aged 36, who had been stabbed too, was taken to St James's Infirmary in a serious condition. A newspaper carried the headline: CURSE AT THE HOUSE OF DEATH. Chapeltown residents had begun complaining about the corner house, which was split into flats. They said a man wielding a knife had attacked one of the occupants of the rooms and when police arrived three people lay on the first floor landing.

Pamela Barker, aged 27, who had been to a cinema with her boyfriend said she had known both Richardson women:

This house just has to be cursed for things like this to happen, I knew Maude Richardson. She used to do my hair and I called her 'Mother'. I also knew Irene Richardson well, and she went from this house to her death. She was a friend of mine. I don't want to be the next one. I've asked the council for a place away from here. Mr Gardiner – we called him 'The Colonel' because all West Indians have nicknames – and Pauline Woofitt were saving up to get married, and you couldn't ever have a cross word with either of them. If you were short of something, they would share it.

Another resident of the house (now replaced by new flats) said: 'Thirteen people live in the flats – but no one stays very long.' Later, Maude Richardson's husband, Myric McNeil Richardson, was jailed for seven years for manslaughter.

Also during that early spring of 1978 police in Leeds and Wakefield were shocked by the sudden death of Detective

Chief Superintendent Dennis Hoban, QPM. Many of his friends had held out the hope that Mr Hoban's tenacity would eventually trap the Ripper, and few would have thought him other than at the peak of health. He was a non-smoker, and at the age of 53 was physically fit. On 10 March he was admitted to Leeds Infirmary with a chest infection. He remained unconscious after an investigative operation, and by 14 March his condition was said to be 'critical'.

He died on 15 March, leaving a widow, Betty, and two sons, and on the day of his funeral, 20 March, an advertisement appeared in the evening newspaper in Leeds, paid for by old lags and criminals who had always respected Dennis Hoban as a 'straight copper'. The message was from 'His old clients and friends. . .'

Later in 1978, forty journalist friends contributed towards a Dennis Hoban Award fund. The award, a silver magnifying glass on a stand, is presented every year for outstanding detective work in West Yorkshire.

chapter nine

Of all the prostitutes slaughtered by the so-called Yorkshire Ripper, 22-year-old Yvonne Ann Pearson was perhaps the most professional in her approach to what was, on occasion, a most remunerative job. She dressed carefully and with style, visited the hairdressers regularly, and was as deft as a fashion model when it came to applying her make-up.

She was a Leeds girl by birth and upbringing, but moved

to a little flat in Woodbury Road in the Heaton area of Bradford in 1974 after she had met and fallen in love with a Jamaican, Roy Saunders. When she first went on 'the game' she tended to solicit in the Manningham red light area of the city. The district contains such places as 'Pie Herberts', a celebrated late-night eating place which specializes in fried chicken, ham shanks, and tripe, as well as pie and mushy peas. Despite its name, 'Pie Herberts' is popular with professional and business people, slumming it after a night on the town.

It was probably her early experience with Bradford free-spenders of this sort which caused her to try her luck further afield. In the next year or so she got into the habit of going 'on tour', travelling to such places as Bristol, Birmingham and Glasgow in search of 'posh' trade, sometimes sleeping with businessmen in their hotels, or going back to flats with them.

By 1977 she was familiar with the London scene, with Shepherd's Market in Mayfair and the conference hotels of Marble Arch and the Edgware Road. Her lissom figure and striking, bleached-blonde hair cut in a page-boy style, gave her a passing resemblance to actress Joanna Lumley of the 'Avengers' TV series and brought plenty of custom her way. Back in Bradford, she even boasted to her friends that she had 'cracked the Arab market'.

But being a professional, she was fully aware of the dangers inherent in her age-old trade. In November 1977 an acquaintance of hers, Jane McIntosh, had been found stabbed to death in a Bayswater hotel bedroom. Mrs McIntosh, originally from Skipton, near Bradford, had also been a top class call girl; her flat in Southampton was sumptuously furnished from the proceeds of vice. Yet all her professional instincts had not saved her from her murderer, who had apparently killed her for her diamond-studded bracelet, money, and various other pieces of jewellery.

Nearer home, Yvonne had often drunk with Tina Atkinson, who had died in the same year as Mrs McIntosh. It was because of these two deaths, both of them indoors, that Yvonne changed her habits and stopped taking men home with her.

'If you think about it,' she told one colleague, 'you have a better chance out on the street. You can at least call for help. If a bloke gets you indoors, you're a gonner.' She also began to carry a pair of long-bladed scissors in her handbag, a potential weapon so popular among street-walkers that it was becoming almost a standard piece of equipment. 'But then again,' she once joked in the Perseverance pub, 'if you're going to get it, there you are. It's just my luck to get knocked on the head.'

There were other risks to the prostitute too, apart from the purely physical ones. As the Ripper's crimes increased, so had the activities of the police, who, having failed to warn prostitutes off the streets, had set out to drive them off, if only for their own good. Twice Yvonne Pearson had been fined heavily for soliciting and shortly after Christmas she had been charged with a third offence. She was bailed to appear before Bradford magistrates on Thursday, 26 January and this time she stood a very good chance of being sent to prison.

This seemed to worry Yvonne far more than the possibility of a murderous attack, mainly because of her children, two-year-old Lorraine and five-month-old Colette. Their father, Roy Saunders, had ended his four year romance with their mother shortly before Christmas and Yvonne had arranged for friends to take care of them should she be sent down.

Despite the looming possibility of prison, Saturday, 21 January found Yvonne Pearson in good spirits. It was a crisp winter morning with a hard blue sky and an invigorating sharpness to the air. Yvonne dressed in black flared slacks, black turtle-neck jumper, and a warm woollen jacket with a bright striped chevron pattern, before setting off down Lumb Lane and turning left towards the clean new pavements of Westgate and the city centre, swinging her big black handbag.

The leather bag contained only a few pounds but, as Yvonne had often joked to friends: 'As long as you're young and fit there's always more where that came from.' In any case she enjoyed her wander around the big department stores like Morrisons of Westgate and after buying the weekend groceries she strolled around the clothing department, riffling through the racks of dresses and trouser suits, feeling the quality of lambswool sweaters and fine cotton blouses. The smell of new cloth, suede, and leather was heady stuff to Yvonne; fashion-conscious as she was it always lifted her spirits.

Back at her flat she unloaded her purchases and counted the few coins in her purse. She felt lively, ready for a night out and lack of money didn't really worry her. She had enough for a couple of drinks. The 16-year-old neighbour who had looked after the children for the afternoon was still sitting in front of the hissing gas fire, gazing at the television screen in one corner of the room. 'Can you stay on for a bit, love?' Yvonne asked. The girl nodded. 'Thanks, love,' said Yvonne. 'I shan't be long.' The children had had their tea and were tucked up in bed. Their mother kissed them lightly so as not to waken them and stepped out into the chilly night air.

Her first stop was the Flying Dutchman; its friendly, noisy atmosphere and lively reggae music were favourites with her. Yvonne sipped her pineapple juice and played a game of pool with a prostitute friend. Just before nine she left, heading for the Perseverance and another quick glass, but there was little to interest her professionally there either.

At a few minutes past nine, she gulped back her drink, nodded good night to the landlady and stepped out into Lumb Lane again. She turned left and left again into the desolate, overgrown waste of Back Southfield Square. It was ill lit and bitterly cold, but the cheerful blare of soul music from the Young Lions Club reassured her. She picked her way diagonally across the square and out into the street lights of the other side, past the raucous Blue Moon Café, the rather more sedate Heaton and Manningham Conservative Club, and the grim-faced Church of Christ Scientist. Here, at 9.30 p.m., she was seen on the corner of Church Lane, waving and shouting cheerily to an immigrant acquaintance across the street . . .

Back at the flat in Woodbury Road, the babysitter sat anxiously watching the clock on the mantelpiece ticking away the hours. Television had long since closed down for the night and there was still no sign of Yvonne. 'I shan't be long,' she had said. The young girl put the latch on the door and settled down to stay the night.

The following morning produced no sign of the missing mother. The babysitter phoned friends of Yvonne and told them what had happened. The friends were the people who were to take in the children if Yvonne was gaoled the following week.

The babysitter was reassured by their reaction to Yvonne's disappearance: 'It's all right, love,' they said. 'She's probably gone to ground – jumped her bail. We'll probably hear from her when she wants to get in touch.'

But nothing was heard that day, or the following. On Tuesday, Yvonne's friends reported her disappearance to the police. Thursday, the day of her scheduled court appearance, came and went, with no sign of her, and though the police suspected that she may indeed have gone to earth in London or one of her other old haunts, they were uneasy.

On 28 January, the Saturday following her disappearance, Detective Inspector John O'Sullivan of Bradford CID issued a brief statement to the press. Yvonne Pearson, he said, had not been back home since she'd left a week previously; she had last been seen in a spot about half a mile from the place where Tina Atkinson had been found butchered in her flat about nine months before. 'We are very concerned about the whereabouts of this girl,' he said. 'We have to keep an open mind about the Ripper.'

A fortnight after Yvonne's disappearance, Helen Rytka was struck down in Huddersfield, and Bradford detectives from the Western Area Task Force were rushed to the site to begin searching for clues. But the murder of Helen only served to intensify fears for Yvonne's safety. Bradford CID enlisted the help of London's Metropolitan Police and several forces in the Midlands to help comb her known haunts in those territories.

In Leeds, her parents, John Pearson a warehouse foreman and his wife Rose, were frantic with worry as a story about their missing daughter flanked the front page splash on the Rytka killing in the *Evening Post*.

Speaking at their Dorset Street home, Mr Pearson told a reporter:

My wife and I are going through hell waiting for Yvonne to get in touch. I have been told that she has been seen in a Leeds pub and that she has been seen in London. I cannot believe she is dead. I don't know why she has decided to disappear, although she was having domestic trouble. I don't want to know where she is living if she doesn't want to tell me. All I want to know is that she is safe. Both my wife Rose and I are horribly upset. I would just ask Yvonne to write to us, send a telegram, do anything to let us know she is OK. Please, just let us know you are alive.

In fact the Pearsons were to have another eight weeks of suspense before hearing any news and when news came it was of the worst kind. A short distance away from Church Street, where Yvonne had last been seen, was Arthington Street, a derelict area with a tract of wasteland used as a cross between a rubbish dump and an unauthorized children's playground and flanked by a bakery and a garage.

On Sunday morning, 26 March, a man was taking a short cut across the lot when he saw a human arm protruding from beneath an upturned, abandoned sofa. At first he thought it was a tailor's dummy; gingerly he moved forward for a closer look and the sickly sweet stench of decay made him run for the garage and a telephone box.

The body had been covered in torn-up turves of grass, soil, rubble, and finally the sofa frame, which had remnants of its khaki-coloured velour still clinging to it. Detective Superintendent Trevor Lapish was one of the first officers at the scene and saw the protruding arm clearly as he approached. Even as he made his first cautious examination he began to ponder a problem which had immediately occurred to him; as he put it later: 'It is difficult to envisage that people came within yards of the settee and didn't see what I saw when I came to the site.'

Children played constantly on the land, climbing over the litter of rubbish. Surely no one, even the youngest child, could have spotted the body and not told someone about it. So the hand had to have been exposed, either by the killer, returning to the scene of the crime, or by a curious dog. Mr Lapish was inclined to the latter theory, but he could not be sure: the Ripper had returned to at least one of his victims, Jean Royle in Manchester, to make sure she would be discovered. But was this a Ripper victim?

Professor David Gee arrived to supervise the removal of the sofa and other material. It was not a pleasant task; the body had lain in the open for two months, and whoever had carried out the deed had been thorough; the face and head had been smashed to a pulp. Some of the clothing was still in position, while other items, including the black leather handbag, were found close by. The hands were sufficiently incorrupt to yield fingerprints and most of the teeth were still in the jaws. From these, the body was positively identified that same afternoon as that of Yvonne Pearson and a ring on her finger confirmed the finding.

Professor Gee took a total of almost twenty-four hours over the post-mortem examination. His findings puzzled both himself and the police; the beating to the head had not been carried out with the Ripper's normal instrument. Instead, 'something like a large stone' had been used. The wounds reminded Professor Gee of those suffered by another Bradford woman, Miss Carole Wilkinson, who had been battered about the head with a 56-lb coping stone the previous year. Her subsequent death, when her life-support machine had been switched off, had made world headlines; later a man was arrested and charged with her murder. Mr Lapish had another fear:

We are very aware of the possibility that this could have been a copycat type murder, someone trying to emulate the so-called Ripper or simply trying to throw us off his track by making it look like the other murders. We have not forgotten that within days of the 'Black Panther' Donald Neilson being arrested, someone set out to try and beat his record. The Guisley student, Mark Rowntree, stabbed four people to death in eight days and was later jailed for life. Some people get unhinged at the thought of publicity. It may well be that we have such a person who, having seen the publicity, has decided to jump on the band-wagon. As a result of Professor Gee's post mortem, we are able to say that this murder is not in all probability one of the prostitute murders already under investigation. The injuries do not coincide.

Once again a massive police operation got under way, with leave stopped, Task Force men drafted in, house-to-house inquiries taking place and spot checks of road traffic in the area carrying on continuously, night and day. But with the Rytka inquiry still in full swing, the police were woefully stretched. Deputy Chief Constable Austin Haywood calculated that they were 'realistically' about 1,500 men short. Nevertheless, morale was high.

'Our resolve is still as strong as ever,' said a young detective constable. 'Every copper working on the Ripper case wants to be the one to feel the bastard's collar. I just wish it could be me. The officer who arrests him will be made for life.'

For by now, a few days after the body's discovery, police policy had changed again. George Oldfield had said that he was 'keeping an open mind'. But soon, officers were talking about Yvonne as a definitie Ripper victim. 'New evidence has turned up,' said one. With hindsight it would seem that that evidence was possibly contained in one of the two letters sent to Mr Oldfield by the Ripper at about that time.

One man who was 'out of the frame' as suspect was Roy Saunders, Yvonne's former lover. He had been in Jamaica from early January and had flown back to Bradford a few days before the body was found. Plainly upset, he told how his four-year romance with the dead woman had turned sour only weeks before. 'We hadn't been happy together for a while,' he said, 'and we had an understanding that if either of us wanted someone else, that was OK. After all, I never put a ring on her finger. But I can't understand why anyone would want to kill her. She never harmed anyone.' Mr Saunders took his two daughters away for a rest shortly after his statement.

One man who did know what it was like to be a prime suspect was stocky, moustached, 37-year-old Terence Hawkshaw, a taxi driver, who lived in the village of Drighlington, in the centre of the 'Ripper triangle' of Leeds, Bradford, and Huddersfield. He had been questioned with other taxi drivers after the death of Tina Atkinson; now he was picked up again. He recalled later: 'They questioned me for days on end and nearly convinced me I was out of my head. When I came out of the police station at Wakefield, I wondered whether I was some kind of Jekyll and Hyde.' He said that when George Oldfield sat behind his desk and gave the opinion that he thought you might be the Ripper it turned your stomach over.

The police visited Mr Hawkshaw's home and with his permission searched it from top to bottom. They checked his car, his garage and his garden. 'They even looked through the dustbin,' he said. 'Then I was asked to go to Wakefield and I was there from 8 p.m. on a Friday to 8 p.m. on Saturday. They gave me blood tests and took clippings of my hair. It got to the stage where I thought they were trying to say: "You can confess and make it easy for yourself. We won't be hard on you." They didn't use those words, but it seemed that that was what they were suggesting.' Finally, the officers thanked him and told him he was free to go: they were satisfied of his innocence. 'I can see that they were only doing their job,' said Mr Hawkshaw, 'and it seemed to me that they were doing it very thoroughly.'

One of the hopeful lines of inquiry arose out of Yvonne's cream and gold address book, found near her body, with its list of thirty-six names and addresses. Detective Superintendent Lapish announced the discovery of the book and gave the men named in it an opportunity to come forward of their own accord, 'so as to save them the embarrassment of a policeman knocking at their door'.

All thirty-six were interviewed and cleared. Woman Police Constable Lena Markovic, a 21 year old who had only joined the Force ten months previously, donned Yvonne's clothes on 3 April and, wearing a page-boy blonde wig over her own dark hair, walked the last known route taken by Yvonne; she was followed by police officers, including an Asian-speaking detective. The experiment, to jog the public memory, produced several lines of inquiry, but few of them added much to the sum total of police knowledge. Yvonne Anne Pearson had become just another name on the unsolved Ripper file.

But her death did have one beneficial result, however small. Her friend Donna Dent, a 23 year old who had sometimes looked after her children and who was Yvonne's close companion on 'the game', appeared before Bradford magistrates in April, in the same dock in which the dead woman was to have stood, on charges of soliciting. She admitted two charges of soliciting and told the court that she was giving up. 'The death of Yvonne came as a tremendous shock to her,' said her solicitor. 'She, like lots of other girls, has decided to quit since the death of her friends Tina Atkinson and Yvonne.' The magistrates gave her a three months suspended sentence.

About this time, however, Vera Millward, who was taking no heed of police warnings, risked her life – as one of Manchester's four hundred prostitutes – once too often. On Wednesday, 17 May, 1978 it was discovered that the Yorkshire Ripper had once again crossed the Pennines to Manchester and chosen to make her his tenth kill.

Vera Millward's body was discovered in the grounds of Manchester's Royal Infirmary by a gardener, Mr Jim McGuigan. As he parked his landscaping firm's van he saw it huddled again a chain-link fence on a rubbish pile in the corner of the car park behind the private patients' home. 'I thought it was a doll or something, at first,' he said. Her body was fully clothed and there were two packets of cigarettes in her pocket, one containing seven cigarettes and the other seventeen. She had received savage head injuries and stab wounds in the stomach and was identified as Vera Millward from her fingerprints. Later it was confirmed that the murderer had been named as the Yorkshire Ripper.

Thus had come to an end the sad life that 40-year-old Vera Millward had spent in turmoil, childbearing and sordidness. Pope John XXIII once said: 'Any day is a good day to be born and any day is a good day to die', but to have been born a girl in Madrid in 1937 was not to have won the lottery for a good life. Vera's first memory was the sound of the bombardment by Franco's victorious army, to be followed, throughout 1938, by the sounds of the execution squads. *Madrilenas* trembled in fear while the vengeance threats, the *limieza*, or 'cleaning', were carried out by the Nationalists.

After the round-up of thousands of Republican prisoners and the sealing of the frontiers with France and Portugal so that none could escape Franco's revenge, there followed the 'lean and hungry years' throughout Spain. The roots of grass were sold as food on market stalls and Spanish children cried themselves to sleep with hunger every night. The lean years for Spain lasted throughout the Second World War, and it was not until the 1950s when tourism began booming as an industry that hundreds of Spanish workers left to be *gastarbeiter* or 'guest-workers' in Germany and to work as waiters and domestic servants in France and England. One of them was Vera. She used to laugh at a Spanish phrase those workers had. They told their British employers: 'You go to our country to play – we come to your country to work.' Wages were low and times were hard, especially for Vera who lived in Manchester with her husband and five children. When the youngest child was fifteen, Mr Millward died, the family split up and Vera, in desperation, turned to prostitution.

She used the names Anne Brown and Mary Barton and yet did not escape a series of convictions. She was last fined in Manchester in November 1973. A former vice-girl said after the murder: 'I used to work the streets with her. Our beat was the Moss Lane, Denmark Road area on Moss Side, but that was two years ago, and I haven't had much contact with her since then.' The prostitutes who work this area take their clients to one of two places, both near hospitals – the Southern Cemetery site, where Scotch Jean was murdered, and near the grass and flower beds of the car park at the Royal Infirmary. Here Vera Millward's body was found in May 1978.

Not long earlier she had told friends that she did not think she had long to live. She had only one lung, and had undergone three major operations in 1976 and 1977. She weighed only 8 st 5 lb, and looked desperately ill, frail and tired. She was wracked with stomach pains and was having treatment for them.

On the night of Tuesday, 16 May, Vera shut behind her the door of the flat where she lived with 49-year-old Jamaican Cy Burkett and their two children aged 6 and 8. She bought two packets of Benson and Hedges cigarettes and then looked hopefully up and down the street. For five years now she had been meeting a man friend regularly every week. He would flash the lights of his white Mercedes near her front door and she would go off in the car with him.

But on this particular night the arrangement went wrong and her once-a-week date failed to turn up. Instead of returning to the flat which was in Grenham Avenue, Hulme – a mile from the home of Jean Royle – Vera decided to seek another client. She never lived to reveal who he was.

A man told the police later that at 1.15 a.m. on Wednesday he had been taking his son to the Royal Infirmary and he believed he had heard Mrs Millward's dying screams. 'There were three screams – each just the one word "help" – then silence.' Apparently no one else had heard them. 'The trouble with this whole area,' said Detective Chief Superintendent Jack Ridgeway, 'is that a scream in the night is not unusual.'

An hour and a half after Vera had left the flat Cy Burkett became worried about her not having returned. He went out to look for her but he soon had to return because he had left the two children alone in the flat.

After the discovery of the body, Mr Ridgeway, head of Manchester CID, arranged for the usual inch-by-inch search of the surrounding area and marks revealed that Mrs Millward's body had been dragged over some gravel to the rubbish pile after she had been beaten to death. The police took a *moulage* – plaster casts of the tyre skid marks in the car park. They contacted Cy Burkett, who saw her body in the mortuary. 'It was a terrible shock. It broke my heart,' he said.

Police also interviewed the man Vera Millward had been supposed to meet on Tuesday night. He told police that their arrangement was that she would sleep with him once a week but as a friend rather than on a professional basis. He said he had taken pity on her and gave her gifts of food for the children and small amounts of money to supplement her family allowance.

Soon after Vera's death Cy Burkett, who had lived with her for nine years, packed up the two children's clothes and left with them for Jamaica and has not returned.

On 24 May, 1978 Manchester detectives went to Leeds to meet West Yorkshire detectives of the newly formed Ripper Squad headed by Detective Chief Superintendent John Domaille. For nearly a year after the Millward killing they spent long hours investigating the ten deaths, while the Ripper laid low.

Then, in the spring of 1979, he struck again.

chapter ten

Whatever repetitive forces history had steeped by battle or legend into the grey stones and green English fields of Halifax, they were at work with a vengeance when nineteen-year-old Josephine Whitaker set off to walk across

Savile Park playing fields just before midnight on wet and snowy 5 April, 1979, to die at the hands of the Yorkshire Ripper.

Josephine was within yards of her home in Ivy Street, when she was struck down with a hammer blow from behind and then dragged away from the street lights of Free School Lane and stabbed time and time again in the chest and stomach, to be left like a bundle of old clothing in the wet grass.

Four hardened detectives turned away from the sight and then covered the body with a polythene tent. Each of them, Assistant Chief Constable George Oldfield, Detective Superintendent Dick Holland, Detective Chief Superintendent Trevor Lapish, all from Yorkshire, and Detective Chief Superintendent Jack Ridgeway from Lancashire, had seen the ghastly work of the Ripper too often before.

The news of Josephine's murder hit the quiet, respectable town when its 90,000 citizens had scarcely begun to recover from one of the harshest English winters in memory: seven months of snow, ice, blizzards, burst pipes and mayhem on the roads. Halifax has some of the steepest hills in Yorkshire and many of its roadways are still cobbled; driving through the wintry conditions had been nightmarish. For this reason alone and the fact that the town had no red light area like its near neighbours Huddersfield and Bradford, it had seemed unlikely that the frenetic Yorkshire killer in his ageing car would chose it as a venue.

Not that the town had been unused to bloodshed in its distant past. The very name was said to stem from the Old English 'Halig Fax' – 'Holy Hair'. Legend had it that a virgin with hair the colour of straw had been beheaded by her importunate suitor; her friends had buried the body but had hung the beautiful flaxen head upon a yew tree, where it remained without decomposing, an object of pilgrimage.

In more recent years, the people of Halifax had divided

their loyalties between the two factions in the English Civil War – the Royalists and Parliamentarians. In the locality there were two regiments led by kinsmen, Sir John Savile of Lupset and Savile of Howley: one for the King, the other against him. In 1642 a battle took place at a spot named Halifax Bank, which was afterwards known as 'Bloody Field' before being renamed after the Saviles as Savile Park. After April 1979 it seemed that the site might more appropriately have kept its old name.

The citizens of Halifax were stunned and shocked by the murder in their midst. They hurried home before it got dark and locked their doors. No one came out, not even to exercise their dogs. In daylight they passed by the tent set up as a command post by Chief Superintendent Frank Storey and Superintendent Alan Stoneley of Halifax police headquarters, as the Ripper Squad's men from Leeds, Wakefield, Bradford and Manchester began to piece together the last hours and minutes of Josephine Whitaker, the nice, quiet girl who had gone to work the day before as a clerk in the largest and most famous Building Society in Britain: the Halifax. They asked themselves: 'Why us? Why Halifax? We have no red light area, no prostitutes. Why pick on us?'

During their inquiries into attacks on fifteen women and the brutal murder of ten of them, before Josephine, the police had not received the kind of help they would have liked. In the red light areas of Leeds and Bradford and Manchester, most people had preferred to keep silent. The prostitutes themselves were, after all, assisting with the crime by allowing a complete stranger to pick them up in a car and take them to the loneliest, quietest spot they knew and where they could not be seen, thus setting the scene for the perfect murder.

Mr George Oldfield, the gruff and stolid Yorkshire detective once more in charge of the inquiries, appealed to the people of Halifax. Then the telephones started to ring in police headquarters as the law-abiding citizens of Halifax rushed forward in their eagerness to help; the police on the hunt for the Ripper had never before experienced such a spontaneous response to their call for information.

The detectives began to look hopefully at each other: descriptions of cars, of people seen that night, of a man seen with Josephine, of the sound of footsteps which could have been hers, of a man trying to pick up a woman earlier that evening of 4 April, came flooding in. The picture began to take shape and they suddenly knew more about the Ripper than they had ever known before: his approximate age, his height, his hair colour, the way he dressed, his boot size, the type of old 'banger' he drove, the area he came from (Sunderland), the area he lived in (West Yorkshire), the workbench tools he used to beat and hack his victims in a frenzy of bloodlust. There were reports from motor-vehicle experts, handwriting experts and psychiatrists which confirmed what they already suspected: that they were dealing with a cunning, aggressive psychopath who would go on killing until he was either caught or he killed himself by his own hand. They also knew, from clues, that he worked as an engineer.

The police uncovered more clues in the respectable town of Halifax than anywhere else, once the people who knew Josephine had recovered from their fear and anguish. As one man wrote to their highly respected local newspaper, the *Evening Courier*: 'When I spoke to one of the girl's workmates she said that the girls in her department were walking around like zombies because they are so grief-stricken. She was truly a nice girl . . .'

Josephine Anne Whitaker was born in Bradford, but she was christened at St Jude's Church, Halifax, near the home of her grandparents, Tom and Mary Priestley. When she was a baby she and her mother, Avril, lived with them at their home in Huddersfield Road, Halifax, and her grandparents always referred to 'Jo' as 'the apple of our eye'. Her hobby as a young girl had been horse-riding, and she loved the open air. In 1972 while she was a pupil at Highlands School, Halifax, her mother married Mr Haydn Hiley, a 40-year-old bricklayer, and 'Jo' and her two brothers, Michael, aged 15, and David, aged 13, moved to the family home in Ivy Street, just off the Savile Park playing fields, a short bus ride into the centre of Halifax.

Josephine grew into an attractive, dark-haired girl of 5 ft 8 ins and she began work as a clerk in the Halifax Building Society. When she went to work there, they told her the history of their firm with great pride: that the Halifax was the biggest building society in the world, with assets of more than £8,000 million and was currently helping more than a million people in Britain to buy their own homes. The Halifax, an early symbol of Yorkshire thrift, stood rock-firm in a county where over half the houses are owner-occupied.

Josephine had seen a lot of a young man called Craig Midgley when she was sixteen and he was seventeen, and she went frequently to his parents' home in Gibbet Street, Halifax. Those grey stones which she passed on her way up the hill from her office to his home were steeped in history, for the street where he lived had been named after the Halifax Maiden, a gibbet dating from 1541, which stood, like a ghostly scene from the French Revolution, on the right-hand side of Gibbet Street.

This horrific guillotine had caused the saying amongst travellers and sailors fearing the Press Gang: 'From Hell, Hull and Halifax, the Good Lord Delivers Us.' The ancient law of the Forest of Hardwicke, in which Halifax parish lay, stated that anyone stealing goods to the value of thirteen and a half pennies or above was subject to a statutory death penalty on conviction. If found guilty, the condemned were taken on the third market day after conviction to a hill known as Gibbet Hill and executed by the machine known as the Halifax Maiden. It stood on a stone platform four feet high and thirteen feet square, with five stone steps leading up to it. The instrument itself consisted of two wooden grooved uprights, fifteen feet high and joined with a cross-beam at the top. Into the grooves was slotted a heavy block of wood four and a half feet long, into the underside of which was fitted an iron axe-head weighing seven pounds twelve ounces. The bailiff was town gaoler, chief magistrate, keeper of the axe and executioner, but the principle of the machine was that no one man was directly responsible for the felon's death – a concept carried into French revolutionary times by Dr Joseph Guillotin, who advocated a similar engine to be used for execution.

The last execution had taken place in 1650 and shortly afterwards Gibbet Hill became a rubbish heap. It was not until the mid-nineteenth century that the platform was excavated from under the rubble. In 1974 the local authorities built an exact replica of the Gibbet and slotted it into the old platform, where it still stands.

It was past this grisly sight that Josephine Whitaker walked to meet her fiancé and spend happy evenings with him and his parents, who had taken to her as one of the family.

On the morning of 4 April, 1979, which was to be Josephine Whitaker's last day alive, she was as carefree and happy as always. She had one special reason to be pleased, for through the post that morning she had received a £60 silver watch, which she had bought through a mail order firm. She wanted to show it to her grandparents and although she never usually visited them on a Wednesday – she went to see them every Sunday – she decided to show them the watch.

Her grandmother was out at an event at St Andrews Church and did not return to Huddersfield Road until 11 p.m. With her grandfather, Tom, she had watched

TV and when the couple, both in their seventies, tried to persuade her to stay the night she laughed and said: 'I'll be all right. I'm not afraid of walking home in the dark.'

Tom Priestly said he would accompany her, but he was suffering from emphysema, a painful chest complaint, and again Josephine laughed at their fears and said: 'I've got to get home, anyway, because the box for my contact lenses is at home, and I have to take them out before I go to sleep. Don't worry, I'll be all right. I'll go the short cut across the playing field. I'll be home in ten minutes.'

The time was 11.40 p.m. when Josephine, wearing her smart outfit consisting of a multi-coloured skirt with white lace trimming, pink jumper, heather-mixture hacking-jacket and tan court shoes with stacked heels, shouted 'goodnight' to her grandparents and walked off into the dark. It was the last time they were to see her alive.

She had no fear of the dark streets near her grand-parents' house; she had walked them many times before and had never been a nervous type of person in any case. One of the things she enjoyed was reading horror stories. Besides, as she had said, it was only ten minutes walk to Ivy Street, across the playing field.

She turned right into Dry Clough Lane from Hudders-field Road, taking the direct diagonal route into Skircoat Moor Road. There were people and cars about, near Savile Park Lodge, which the locals called the Refreshment House, where cups of tea were served and toilets were open late. At this time of night people exercised their dogs on the grass, often staying in their cars and leaving the door open and the light on for the dog to return after a run on the grass.

The light rain and sleet of the early evening had cleared. The grass was wet, but she was wearing good, strong leather shoes. She would be home before the clock at St Jude's and the other one in the distance, at Crossley and Porter

School, chimed midnight and she could check her new silver watch against them. Looming near the school clock was an even more prominent landmark against the night sky: the Wainhouse ornamental tower, originally built as a chimney to a dye-works, an early attempt to cure Halifax's terrible smoke pollution problem, and in front of that, on the field itself, two rugby goalposts silhouetted against the sky . . .

The man who calls himself the new Jack the Ripper, who always operates by night and travels by car, saw Josephine walking alone. He had almost been caught by a police constable in the Chapeltown area of Leeds, and he knew that both that and Bradford's red light district were no longer easy hunting ground for his prey. Many of the prostitutes had been frightened off the streets. Some had gone abroad or into brothels and the police were active, checking every car, questioning any motorist kerb crawling and any man loitering after dark.

Even Manchester, where he had killed two prostitutes, was too 'hot' an area for him and when he had written letters to the police and to a newspaper he had led them astray deliberately by returning to Halifax. He had probably read in the newspapers that they thought him to be very cunning. Every newspaper in Britain had written about him, and in the summer of 1977 reporters had come from America to write about his killing in Leeds . . . now there was a £25,000 reward on his head.

Josephine Whitaker's body was found by Mrs Jean Markham, who was on her way to work at the confectioner's firm of Rowntree Mackintosh and was standing at the bus stop in Savile Park Road at 6.30 a.m. on 5 April. 'I thought it was just a bundle of rags until I saw a shoe lying nearby,' she said. 'I went across the road and was just about to pick up the shoe when I realized someone was lying there.' She bent down to touch Josephine and then saw that she was dead and ran home to Green Terrace Square, where she screamed down the telephone at the police: 'There's a body in the park.' Within minutes the local police arrived and she took them to the scene. The police sealed off the area around Josephine's body on the football pitch. Her brown shoe lay thirty feet away.

A bus driver, Ronald Marwood, had seen the 'bundle of rags' at 5.30 a.m. when he drove the No. 6, the first bus of the day, past the spot. He reported it to the bus depot, but Metro Calderdale did not pass his message on to the police. They realized their driver must have seen a body when the police telephoned at 7.20 a.m. to ask them to move the bus stop on Savile Park away from the scene of the crime and the eyes of the curious who were queueing to go to work.

Josephine's younger brother, 13-year-old David, her favourite whom she often took to the cinema, had gone to collect the newspapers for his paper round at 6.30 a.m. and as he returned across the playing fields he saw the police activity. Out of curiosity he went to look, saw a body covered up and was horrified to see one of Josephine's brown shoes a few yards away.

He ran home to tell his step-father Haydn Hiley what he had seen. Josephine's mother, who had not waited up the night before as Josephine had her own key to the house, checked her room and found it empty. They rang the police, distraught with grief.

The Halifax police had contacted the special Ripper Squad and senior detectives began their journey from Wakefield, Leeds, Bradford and Manchester, and a telephone call was made to Professor Gee, the pathologist. Tracker dogs were brought to Savile Park playing fields and police officers began an inch-by-inch search of the grass. Passers by who saw the line move across the field started another of the hundreds of rumours which had begun when the Ripper had started his killings four and a half years before. 'They're looking for a contact lens,' they said.

But they were wrong, for Josephine's contact lenses – the reason for her hurrying home the night before – were in place and, perhaps even more ironic, the new silver watch on her wrist was still ticking the time away.

Police began to question everyone going towards the bus queue or going to work by car, motor-cycle or bicycle, and to make house-to-house inquiries around Ivy Street, Josephine's home. Cautiously, Detective Chief Superintendent Trevor Lapish told reporters:

We will not know the cause of death until after examination later today. It could have been a road accident. There are scuff marks indicating that she might have been dragged and with her being found so close to the road, she might have been dragged from a car across the grass.

As officials of the bus company moved the bus stop further down the road, students at the Crossley and Porter School were told that a body had been found on the pitch where their lacrosse match was due to be held that morning and the match had been cancelled.

Soon afterwards Professor Gee began his first inspection before supervising the removal of Josephine's body to the nearby Royal Infirmary, a few yards down from St Jude's Church. A hush descended on the area around the playing fields. A patrol van stood in Free School Lane with its radio chattering; the hundred officers now engaged in the hunt for Josephine's killer asked countless people: 'Were you in this area between the hours of eleven o'clock last night and two o'clock this morning? Did you see anything unusual, notice any parked cars, loiterers, or drivers kerb crawling?'

The next morning, 6 April, while Professor Gee continued his examination of the body, reporters swarmed into the area from Leeds, Bradford, Manchester and London, including foreign correspondents based in England. Radio and television reporters interviewed the inhabitants of

Halifax, who tended to brush questions aside and hurry on towards their homes or places of work. Josephine's firm said that she had just been promoted and given a rise in her department. The wife of the proprietor of the Tower House Hotel, Washer Lane, Halifax, where Josephine had started part-time work as a barmaid to save up for the silver watch, described her as a quiet girl who got on with her work and did not speak unless she was spoken to.

Her former fiancé, Craig Midgley, aged 20, said he was too shocked to see anyone that day and stayed away from his work at Philips Electrical to be with his parents in Gibbet Street. Later on he was to talk about Josephine's deep feeling for her grandparents.

They were very very special to Josephine and she loved them deeply. During the two years I went out with her we went there to tea every Sunday. You could see there was a very special bond between them. She loved all her family and they all made me feel very welcome. I just don't know what they must be going through. Josephine was confident and fearless. When she came to visit my family, who all liked her tremendously, she would say she would walk into town for a bus, but I would never let her. Josephine had a great love of life. Her ambition was to be happy. She really enjoyed meeting people and was very popular, with a lot of friends. There was nothing she liked more than a night out in Halifax among people. She was an outgoing girl who liked all the things a normal girl of nineteen likes – dancing, clothes and having fun. She loved her work. She was very clever and bright, a very generous and kind girl. I met her first of all on a bus, about three years ago, and we got engaged last year. She was more serious, however, and wanted to get married and raise a family, but we knew it wasn't really going to work out, so by mutual agreement we parted in May. I have not seen her since then. I'm absolutely shattered by her death, and so are my workmates, as many of them knew her. It is a tragedy. She did not fear people, so I do not know how she would have reacted if she were attacked. All I know is that she loved life . . .

Neighbours of Josephine's family called to pay their respects and many broke down and sobbed in the deathly silence that hung in the air in the Bell Hall area, where everyone had gone into mourning for Josephine.

Police began contacting members of a party held at Standeven House, Birdcage, Halifax, on the night of 5 April, by the Bradford Pennine Insurance Sports and Social Club when it was reported that one of the guests saw a man running fast down the moor at about 1.15 a.m. Between 140 and 150 people attended the party and all were questioned by police over the next days of intensive inquiry.

The park area was described by one local resident, Mr Glen Cockroft, 21-year-old student: 'It's pretty quiet around here once the pubs have closed. You only get a few people around at night times – mainly walking their dogs.'

Thirty-six hours after Josephine's body was found, Assistant Chief Constable Oldfield announced to the press that one man and one man alone was responsible for her murder – the homicidal maniac who had come to be known as the Yorkshire Ripper. He said: 'The dead girl is perfectly respectable, similar to Jayne MacDonald. It is more than a year since the Ripper last struck in Yorkshire. Josephine was badly beaten about the head and suffered injuries to the body.' No other details as to the state of the body were given and very little else emerged at the inquest. For Professor Gee was a cautious man. Moreover, George Oldfield and his police team had emphasized time and time again to younger detectives not to release details of the killer's *modus operandi* for two specific reasons: if published, telephone calls were invariably received from a lunatic fringe claiming to have committed the crime and if they knew initmate details the police could not eliminate them as nut-cases amongst the mass of informants who rang the incident room; and also as a protection against imitative crime, or 'copycat' killers. Young detectives had also been warned against discussing clues, for if the Ripper knew what the police knew, he might change his tactics, methods, weapons, clothes and car. Some of these clues would be essential evidence in a court of law, to get a conviction.

On 7 April Mr Oldfield made his first appeal for the driver of a car to come forward. The outstanding response by the people of Halifax was bearing fruit. For once, it was thought, the Ripper had made a great mistake. In the red light areas where he had killed previously, even law-abiding residents tended not to notice the many strangers in the streets. But in the respectable residential area of Bell Hall, not only had they remembered strangers, but gave good descriptions, and knew the makes and years of cars. George Oldfield was seeking a white Ford Escort, a pre-1969 model with flared wings, which had been seen driving along Savile Park Road and had stopped outside the café at Savile Park Lodge the night Josephine had been murdered.

More than 200 policemen were now taking part in the investigation, and Mr Oldfield announced that the search of the football pitch had been 'fruitful'. He added:

We are receiving information from people all over the country. We are looking for a clever person who, if he is not living with us, is not far out of West Yorkshire. The man is obviously mentally deranged, but now he has changed his pattern. We cannot stress how careful every woman must be. Unless we catch him, and the public must help us, he will go on and on. I warn all women to use lighted streets and to walk home with someone they know. In no circumstances accept lifts from strangers.

When the *Evening Courier* went on sale on 7 April, nine readers' letters were published, eight of them protesting against the publication of a photograph showing Josephine's body, partly hidden by a cover, but showing her face and right shoulder. It was, said readers, 'flagrant bad taste', 'disgusting sensationalism', 'deplorable lowering of standards'. The odd man out wrote:

I thought how inconsiderate it was, but after a much disturbed night thinking about the incident and her poor family, I think the *Courier* did the right thing. If it upsets the guilty party as much as it upset me, he may as well give himself up, because he will never know peace again as long as he lives.

On Sunday morning, 8 April, at the Palm Sunday service at St Jude's Church, the vicar, the Reverend Michael Walker, asked his packed congregation to adopt a truly Christian attitude and pray for everyone concerned, including the Ripper. 'He needs help,' Mr Walker said, 'he is someone's child, husband or father. Pray not only for Josephine and her family but the Ripper and his family. They may be unwittingly protecting him.' The usual anthem in the church was replaced by a more solemn piece and after prayers the congregation observed a minute's silence. Among them were Josephine's brothers, David, and Michael, who had sung in the choir until his voice broke. Outside the church Mr Walker was asked why he had asked for prayers for the Ripper. He said: 'My prayers were from the heart. I did not prepare them.'

Mr Hiley and Josephine's mother, a schoolteacher, were inundated with messages of sympathy. Mr Hiley said:

All Josephine's family want these people to know just how much these kind thoughts have meant to us. It has touched us deeply to know that people are thinking of us at this time and that we are not on our own. People have been thoughtful and have tried not to disturb us. Teacher friends of my wife, for example, sent a representative of the group. The whole family are just trying to keep busy.

The following Monday, after one of the quietest weekends Halifax had known, the *Evening Courier* printed five more letters of protest about the photograph, with an editorial alongside:

The picture was used in the knowledge that it would shock. It was used in the hope that the message would be driven home that it is unsafe for women to be out late at night unaccompanied, that it may help in speeding justice. Use of the picture was not for 'sensationalism' in the sense that has come to be accepted in newspaper terms, as a titillating stimulant for sales, although it was anticipated that something of a sensation may be created. It was an awful picture of yet another awful crime and was seen by the editor, who acknowledges responsibility for its use, as part of the newspaper's duty to impart information. It is a duty which is often distasteful. One that sometimes offends.

The police issued details of three cars which had been seen parked in and around Savile Park on the night Josephine was murdered. They also issued a photofit of a man they wanted to interview, and this picture was later to hinder police inquiries, as readers of newspapers were given the impression that, instead of the man being sought in the normal process of elimination, the picture was definitely that of the Ripper.

The man, who had been seen driving a dark-coloured Ford Escort saloon through Halifax town centre at 9 p.m. on Wednesday night, was described as having been: white, aged about 30, of scruffy appearance, average height and build, with collar-length dirty blond hair which covered his ears and curled at the ends. He had a square-shaped face and jaw, and Jason King style moustache, not well trimmed and coming halfway down his chin. He was wearing a tartan checked, heavy, brushed-cotton shirt open halfway down the front and a tartan lumber jacket with a light-coloured fur collar. The car was made between 1968 and 1975 and would therefore have the suffix G to N on the registration plate. It was dirty and had old-style wings.

Mr Oldfield warned the public not to concentrate solely on this man but to try and recall anyone else in the area at the time and added that they were looking for two other cars: a dark-coloured Datsun, possibly an estate car, seen at midnight, unoccupied and without lights, and a new wedge-shaped Rover, orange or tan coloured, seen parked outside the Refreshment Rooms.

Mr Oldfield was also following a lead which had come from the occupants of Savile Park Lodge, who had told police questioners that they had heard the running footsteps of a woman, going into the toilet at the back of the Refreshment Rooms, between 12.10 and 12.15 a.m. on Thursday. Mr Oldfield said: 'The footsteps could have been Josephine's. We want to know if anyone else remembers going to the toilets at about that time.'

On 10 April, police announced that they had been told by a Halifax woman that she had been propositioned by a man in the Ford Escort and he resembled the man in the photofit picture she had seen in the newspaper. Oldfield said: 'She left work in the town centre and was on her way home, going to the bus stop, when she was propositioned by this man. When he saw the woman's reaction, he quickly drove away.' The woman's identity was kept secret.

Another woman, Marilyn Moore from Leeds, whose new address in a Yorkshire mill town was kept secret, also saw the photofit, and said to reporters: 'That's the man who attacked me. I still dream about the swine.'

On 14 December, 1977 Marilyn, then aged 25, had been found battered and bleeding, with a fractured skull, after having been violently attacked and beaten about the head in Leeds. The attack had taken place near a beck (small stream) just off Buslingthorpe Lane, known to be a local 'lovers' lane'. She had left home in Harehills at 6 p.m. intending to return at 11 p.m. and had accepted a lift from a man in a maroon car who was cruising in Leopold Street, Chapeltown. Although only 5 ft, she fought with her attacker, but was left for dead with a head wound that required 56 stitches. She was in hospital for two weeks and police at her bedside were given this description of the assailant: about 25 to 28, wearing a blue or black zip-up coat, yellow shirt, blue jeans and speaking with an accent that was not local. He was about 5 ft 6 ins and had a Jason King style moustache.

After recovering in hospital, Marilyn Moore had left the Yorkshire area, so as not to have to live in fear and dread that one day her attacker might put her through the horrific experience again. She moved around from town to town, seeking anonymity, finally taking a job as a full-time mill worker, and settling down with her two children, aged 6 and 12 months.

At her secret address she said:

I still live in fear of that man. I must have come back from the dead after he attacked me. He had the same eyes, eyebrows, nose, the face is the same. It's the same guy. I moved around the country because I was terrified. I am frightened that he will come for me because I can identify him. I am the first person the police will come to if anyone is arrested. I remember he had a very thin beard. Maybe he hadn't shaved. He also had fairly broad shoulders and big hands and a sun-tanned face.

Although the description given of her attacker by Marilyn Moore had similarities with the one issued from Halifax in April 1979, the police had no particular reason to suppose either was a description of the Ripper and they had never said so. Mr Oldfield stressed that the photofit picture was only of a man police wished to talk to in order to eliminate him from their inquiries, but the press had misinterpreted it.

The result of this confusion over the photofit picture was that police instructed newspaper editors to put a red sticker on all photo files on the Ripper indicating that no photofit pictures were to be published. But even in the late summer of 1979 London papers continued to print this misleading picture.

Soon afterwards a man came forward with a new lead: he had seen a girl whose description tallied with that of Josephine, walking with a man near Savile Park on the night of the murder. He had seen them, he told detectives, 'side by side' at about 11.40 p.m., walking up Manor Heath Road from Skircoat Green Road to Savile Park.

Mr Oldfield said:

First we have to establish whether or not it was Josephine and whether this man is the chap we are looking for. The man could have been her murderer, or he could have left her before she was attacked. The witness saw nothing untoward. The couple appeared to have been walking together. There were a lot of people around Savile Park at the time, including an off-duty policeman, believed to have been walking his dog, shortly before or after Josephine was murdered.

He added that the man seen walking by the playing field with the girl did not fit the description of the other man they wanted to interview, who had propositioned the woman in Halifax.

Meanwhile, after thorough study of the report by Professor Gee, plus the reports which had been sent by the forensic science laboratory at Wetherby, Mr Oldfield felt confident enough to say that Halifax had produced the best leads yet in the murder hunt for the Ripper. He held a press conference to announce that they were seeking an engineering worker with connections in the north east of England – he had received letters from the Ripper postmarked in that area – and he knew far more than ever before about Britain's public enemy number one.

The pathologist and the forensic team had confirmed that the eleventh victim of the Ripper bore slight traces of the type of oil or grease used in certain engineering work and Mr Oldfield said: 'The man we are seeking is an artisan or manual worker, either skilled or semi-skilled, with engineering or mechanical connections. He is possibly a skilled machine tool fitter, electrical or maintenance engineer.'

The letters, sent to Mr Oldfield and signed 'Jack the Ripper' had all been postmarked in the same area and in his appeal to engineering firms to check on the movement of their workers between West Yorkshire and the north east, he specified these dates when the Ripper was there: 7 or 8 March, 1978; 12 or 13 March, 1978; and 22 or 23 March, 1979. The last one had arrived at his headquarters in Wakefield only eleven days before the Ripper murdered Josephine Whitaker in Halifax.

Mr Oldfield also asked firms in Yorkshire for details of employees who were off work on those dates and for information from companies in the north east where employees from Yorkshire were engaged in maintenance, repair or installation work on their premises on any of those dates.

From each murder we have gained a little bit more, and we have gained quite a bit from the Halifax murder. We now believe the Ripper is a white male, aged between 30 and 55 and of average or above average height. In all probability he lives alone or with aged parents or parent.

Laconic as always, Mr Oldfield did not go into further detail, nor did he take newspapermen into his confidence about the special clues they had found in Halifax.

The officers of Task Force in Halifax continued to work twelve to fifteen hours a day and gave up their Easter leave. When Mr Oldfield, known to the officers on the Whitaker case as 'The Guvnor', had casually announced that he was looking for an engineer, he had not spoken of the enormity of the task: for in England, Scotland and Wales there are more than 2,000,000 engineering workers and the Engineering Employers' Federation has 6,500 companies as members. On Tyneside and in the north east of England alone there are 10,000 engineering firms, and there are 1,250 firms in the Halifax, Huddersfield and Bradford areas.

By slow and dogged process of elimination, the Task Force officers began to sift the mountain of statements and information that began to pour into headquarters. They knew that when the list was narrowed down to a few thousand men, one vital clue could help to identify Jack the Ripper: for he had licked the stamps that he placed on the envelopes to post to Mr Oldfield, and the forensic science laboratory at Wetherby had analysed the saliva and from it pinpointed the Ripper's rare blood group.

What has been the effect on ordinary people of this man about whom the police know so much – and yet so little? In the late summer of 1979, when we visited Halifax, we found that the people in the Savile Park area were still afraid after dark. The Reverend Michael Walker and his wife were doubtful that, when the dark nights came, their parish evening programme would have any attendance at all, and schoolchildren were being escorted to and from school as a precaution. Husbands were refusing to let their wives go anywhere alone and women were going to their doctors for help and pills after having nightmares about the Ripper. Tradesmen were constantly refused admittance to houses – TV repair men, plumbers, glaziers etc. – in case one of them was the Ripper. Taxi drivers were always asked to wait to see their fare to the door before driving on. Dog owners would only exercise their dogs in daylight. Any strange man hanging around at night was suspicious. The Ripper's terrorism had certainly had its effect on the respectable town of Halifax.

chapter eleven

Before the summer of 1979, the London newspapers had not taken much notice of the bizarre story unfolding in Lancashire and Yorkshire. The *Guardian* had given full reports from time to time, but the story had not yet made headlines in Fleet Street for the simple reason that its crime reporters tend to stay on their own 'patch'. But on Tuesday, 26 June, this attitude changed when the police announced that a sensational tape recording, on a cassette, had been sent by the Ripper to Mr George Oldfield. The London *Evening Standard* blazoned the story across its front page: '*I'm Jack – you're having no luck catching me*', with the headline: VOICE OF THE RIPPER.

Police confirmed that the voice on the tape was that of the man who had sent three letters to the police from the north east of England and another letter to the editor of the *Daily Mirror*, Manchester – he was clearly a reader of the northern edition of the *Mirror*, for the edition in the south of England gives the Holborn address.

That evening the arrogant and mocking Geordie voice on the tape was played on radio and television programmes and millions of Britons listened with horror to his boasting and his hollow, humourless laugh at the end. He said:

'I'm Jack. I see you're still having no luck catching me. I have the greatest respect for you, George, but, Lord, you are no nearer catching me now than four years ago when I started. I reckon your boys are letting you down, George. You can't be much good, can ya? The only time they came near catching me was a few months back in Chapeltown when I was disturbed. Even then it was a uniformed copper, not a detective. I warned you in March that I'd strike again. Sorry it wasn't Bradford. I did promise you that, but I couldn't get there. I'm not quite sure when I will strike again, but it will be definitely some time this year, maybe September or October, even sooner if I get the chance. I am not sure where, maybe Manchester. I like it there. There's plenty of them knocking about. They never learn, do they, George? I bet you warned them, but they never listen. At the rate I'm going I should be in the book of records, I think it's eleven up to now, isn't it? Well, I'll keep on going for quite a while yet. I can't see myself being nicked just yet. Even if you do get near, I'll probably top myself first.

'Well, it's been nice chatting to you, George.

'Yours, Jack the Ripper.

'*No good looking for fingerprints. You should know by now it's clean as a whistle.*

'*See you soon. Bye. Hope you like the catchy tune at the end. Ha ha.*'

The tape recording ended with a pop song containing the words 'Thank you for being a friend'. The writing on the envelope the cassette arrived in was the same as in the letters he had already sent which contained details of the crimes that only the Ripper could have known.

After the tape had been broadcast the police arranged for a special telephone number, Leeds 464111, to be set up. Callers dialling it are able to hear the Ripper's recording played back and it is hoped that someone with suspicions of the identity of the murderer will ring in, recognize the voice and report to the police. The number of people who dial it – for whatever reasons – is now so colossal that the number of lines has had to be doubled.

On Saturday, 30 June, the Ripper's letter to George Oldfield, dated 23 March, 1979, was published throughout Britain in an attempt to get someone to recognize the handwriting. The letter, along with the others posted in the north east, had been subjected to intensive tests at Wetherby: a watermark test on the paper and envelope; a post office check to try to place the letter box, timing, and confirm the authenticity of postmark; fingerprint tests inside and outside the envelope and on the writing paper and stamp; a saliva analysis of the gum on the back of the stamp to give the Ripper's rare blood group and confirm that he and only he licked the other stamps; a check on the interior of the envelope for dust and fibres; an ink analysis; and handwriting and educational experts' analyses.

The letter said:

'*Dear Officer. Sorry I haven't written, about a year to be exact, but I haven't been up North for quite a while. I wasn't kidding last time I wrote . . . That was last month so I don't know when I'll get back on the job but I know it won't be Chapeltown – too bloody hot there maybe*

Bradfords Manningham. Might write again if up North. Jack the Ripper.'

Mr Oldfield had deleted a middle section of the letter and refused to go into detail. The missing section follows the words *'last time I wrote'*. Following the murder of Barbara Leach in Bradford, it would appear that this section was his threat to kill in Bradford, for the Ripper said in the tape recording: *'I warned you in March that I'd strike again. Sorry it wasn't Bradford. I did promise you that, but I couldn't get there.'* The Ripper went to Halifax instead and killed Josephine Whitaker.

Police who had raided a house in Alfred Street, Darlington, following a tip-off by suspicious neighbours, questioned a man about a collection of Ripper press cuttings. The CID later said they had been collected by a student preparing a thesis. Police also announced that they would not hesitate to raid homes even if it meant embarrassment after many 'sex secrets' of wayward husbands and boy-friends were telephoned to the headquarters following the broadcast.

During the weekend the Freephone in Leeds was jammed with calls, mostly from 'ghouls' seeking the thrill of hearing the Ripper's voice.

The Ripper tape was played in working men's clubs in the Sunderland area, where 100 police officers were at work on the case. The pop song containing the words 'Thank you for being a friend' was also played in nightclubs and people were asked if they knew anyone who had bought the disc.

Towards the end of July, the strain of working round the clock for two years began to tell on George Oldfield, who had been leading the Ripper inquiry since Jayne MacDonald's murder in July 1977. He became ill and his doctor ordered him to rest. During all that time 'The Guvnor' had had only one day off, when he watched a cricket match in an attempt at relaxation. But from then on, throughout the summer of 1979 and the height of the

Yorkshire cricket season, George Oldfield was given strict orders to 'rest up' for two months.

The police have been working themselves to the limit on this extraordinary and terrifying case, but other less orthodox approaches to the problem have also been tried. During the past four years various clairvoyants have approached the police with help and descriptions. In each case a senior police officer has listened and taken note of the clairvoyant's information, knowing that in the past clairvoyants have been known to produce vital clues. At the time of the Jayne MacDonald murder in Chapeltown, Leeds, clairvoyant Mr Alfred Cartwright of Brander Drive, Gipton, went to the police and told them:

As soon as I saw a picture of this girl I began to see pictures of the man who killed her. He is an ordinary working man, aged about 28 or 30, who lives in Bradford. In four weeks time he will strike again in the Chapeltown area [ten days after this he attacked Mrs Maureen Long in Bradford] but he will then be caught.

Mr Cartwright, medical herbalist, former soldier and judo expert, added: 'This man has trouble sleeping. He is aware of what he has done and it is troubling him. At work he will occasionally be unable to stop shaking.'

A week after the attack on Mrs Long another clairvoyant, Mr Simon Alexander of Mansfield, Nottinghamshire, was taken to five of the murder sites, four in Leeds and one in Bradford. 'I think the first death was probably an accident, after the man was taunted, and it has built up from there. Obviously there is something very wrong with the man, but I don't think he will murder another woman.' The Ripper murdered six more women after this statement.

At the time of the Rytka murder a woman clairvoyant approached the police and said she believed the Ripper lived in a Pennine village, possibly one beginning with the letter 'L'. On 1 July, 1979 Mrs Doris Stokes from London, who had helped the Los Angeles police solve a killing there the week before, made predictions that the Ripper's first name was 'Johnny' or 'Ronnie'; that he was 5 ft 8 ins tall, in his mid-20s to 30s, with dark hair and a scar below his left eye which twitched when he got agitated; she thought he had been treated at a hospital with a 'ch' in its name – possibly Cherry Knowle Hospital at Ryhope, Sunderland; his mother had died of cancer and was called either 'Dolly' or 'Polly'; the town of Gateshead, County Durham, and Bewick Street were important links, she said.

On 26 July, 1979 Manchester astrologer Mr Reginald DuMarius sent his deductions to Mr Oldfield, saying that the Ripper strikes when the moon is positioned in an orbital course of 22 degrees, and 'he will strike tomorrow, Friday, night'. He added: 'I have always deducted that the Ripper was born at 9.30 p.m. on 15 September, 1946 – making him 32 years of age.' There was no attack that Friday.

chapter twelve

Nine weeks after sending his taped message to George Oldfield, the Yorkshire Ripper struck his twelfth victim with what one police officer termed 'breathtaking audacity'. The venue was Bradford again, but this time the site was a good mile away from the heavily policed red light areas of Manningham and Lumb Lane; instead the Ripper chose a spot just three hundred yards from the city's Central Police Station and, for the third time, a respectable girl died.

She was 20-year-old Barbara Janine Leach, a social sciences student at Bradford University.

Barbara Leach was born in Hazel Road, Kettering, on 5 January, 1959, the second child of David Leach, a bank clerk, and his wife Beryl. They lived in a modest pre-war semi-detached house very close to the two schools Barbara was to attend: Henry Gotch School and Southfield Girls' School. Her mother worked in the local telephone exchange until she took a higher education course and became a teacher to help Barbara and her brother Graham, two years older, through school and university. Her father was a well-respected member of the Barclay's Bank staff in Kettering.

With her 'A' levels in English and Religious Knowledge, Barbara had a choice of several universities. She chose Bradford because, in the words of her brother, 'she had a totally cosmopolitan type of feminism'. Barbara Leach wanted to mix with 'real people' and to be part of another world she had never known – public bar cheerfulness, the friendliness of working-class people, and living next to 'the other half' in the back streets of Bradford.

She returned to Bradford early – before the autumn 1979 term started at the university, promising her parents that she would study hard in her third year for her Bachelor of Science degree and saying she would visit them as soon as she had settled back into her flat in Grove Terrace.

Grove Terrace is one of seven quiet streets which run parallel to each other in the wishbone-shaped area between Great Horton Road and Morley Street which leads down-hill to the Bradford police station. Most of the houses in these streets are owned by the university, whose tower block rises from the Great Horton Road campus. They are primly kept stone houses which are now mostly converted into flats and set with neat front gardens and backyard areas reached through narrow passageways. In one of these houses, in the thoroughfare known as Claremont, the composer Delius lived a hundred years ago. Two streets down the hill, Grove Terrace housed Barbara Leach and half a dozen other students.

She had a full existence; besides doing the cooking and cleaning, which she enjoyed, she worked hard at her studies, taking time off only to go riding in the outlying village of Tong, or to join colleagues for drinks at the Bradford Interchange, the Shoulder of Mutton or the Mannville Arms.

On Saturday, 1 September, Barbara remembered that it was her father's 53rd birthday and she had forgotten to send him a birthday card. So she did the next best thing: she telephoned her mother and asked her to apologize on her behalf to her father and to say she would be back in Kettering two days later. She also asked her mother to arrange an appointment with a hairdressing salon in the town. When Barbara rang off and said: 'Bye, see you Monday', she was in high spirits, laughing, joking with her mother and as cheerful as always. It was the last time her mother would hear her daughter's voice.

That Saturday was a hot bright day at the heel of summer, softening to a balmy dusk. As the evening lights flickered on in the Indian and Greek restaurants of Morley Street, rich smells of garlic, curry, fried chicken and grilling kebabs filtered up from Bradford town centre – the 'Jacob's Well' area. Music began to throb from private flats, from dancing clubs such as 'Queenie Roma's' and from the Mannville Arms, popular with students from both Bradford University and the nearby polytechnic for its 'New Wave' selection on the juke box. The Mannville, which serves one of Yorkshire's favourite draught beers – Tetley's – is popular with local youngsters, patronizingly termed 'townies' by the students, and by hardcore punk rockers. But the landlord, Roy Evans, had catered to several generations of students during his tenancy at the house and it was the students who were his favourite customers.

Sometimes, particularly at weekends, he would let a few of them stay behind for 'afters' – that is for drinks after the legal closing time of 11 p.m. – under the rule which allows a landlord to treat personal friends in his own time.

Even so, a student's grant meant that drinks had to be eked out – particularly in the case of 'Babs' Leach, who had been out to lunch on Friday and had a further luncheon date planned for Monday. So it was not until about 9 p.m. that she set out, along with a casual friend and flat-mate Paul Smith, a 21-year-old student, and four other friends on the two-minute walk up Grove Terrace and around the corner to the Mannville.

Fifty or sixty people were already crowding the bar of the Mannville when Bab's group arrived, easing through the crush for pints of Tetley's and halves of lager. Babs, a lively, extrovert girl in company, crisp and trim in her cheesecloth shirt and blue denims with a jokey 'Best Rump' sign on one buttock, made her way to the darts board to put her name down for a game. From the juke box current favourites – Cliff Richard with 'We Don't Talk Anymore' and the haunting, amplified theme from 'The Deer-hunter' – boomed out over and over again.

At 11 p.m. came closing time and the crowd thinned out. Towels were put over the pumps, the juke box was turned down and the main lights extinguished. Only a few students remained behind, some helping the staff by collecting glasses and lending a hand with the washing up. More pints were pulled and the laughter from the little group silhouetted against the bar lights continued for another hour or so.

At 1 a.m. 'afters' were over. There was the usual banter. 'Come on, drink off. We're open again at twelve tomorrow morning. There'll still be beer then, you know!'

Paul, Barbara and a couple of colleagues left the front door and turned into Great Horton Road, walking slowly up the incline. There was some discussion about whether they should go on to an Indian restaurant that stayed open until 2 a.m. but they decided against it. The night out had mellowed them and a light warm drizzle on the soft evening air, with no breath of wind, had a soothing quality of its own. At the corner of Grove Terrace, Barbara hesitated as the others turned left towards the flat.

'Paul,' she said. 'I think I'll just go for a stroll. Can you wait up for me? I lent my key to Gabrielle Rhodes so that she can feed J.C. tomorrow afternoon.' J.C. was a black and white stray kitten which Barbara had taken in; she and her fellow students usually expected to be out and about on Sundays.

Paul nodded and waved a hand. 'I shan't be long,' said Babs, walking on up the hill.

Ash Grove does boast a few ash trees, as well as elms and hawthorns, which line the pavement and lend it a pleasant, suburban air. At night, in summer, the street lamps shine on the underside of the leaves, giving the passer-by the impression of walking under an uneven canopy of green. But between the lights the shadows cluster in densely. Footsteps ring on the pavements to be muffled again by the leaves overhead. There is an odd echo effect. It is easy to imagine that you are being followed, to look around sharply only to find the street empty. Except, perhaps, for the clustered shadows . . .

At first, Paul Smith was not unduly alarmed by Barbara's non-appearance. There were always plenty of parties in the student area and she had many friends. It seemed likely that she might have called in somewhere for a final drink and a dance. Through his window he could hear music coming from the direction of Ash Grove.

But the following morning her bed was still empty, the door still on the latch as he had left it. It was unlike Babs to stay out all night; she had no steady boy-friends, and she was not a 'permissive' type. Paul and friends began making inquiries. Alison Hillman, a 19-year-old engineering student, asked around the university campus, while Paul contacted Gabrielle Rhodes, Barbara's 22-year-old social science student friend who had borrowed the key.

By midday, when the Mannville Arms opened its doors again and Barbara had still not been sighted, the worst fears were lodged in the minds of all her friends. As one said later: 'The consciousness of the Ripper has never been very far from the surface around here for two or three years, but somehow no one ever thought of him striking in Little Horton – the student area. It's so friendly around here.'

The police were not so easily convinced and that Sunday afternoon a search got under way. Gabrielle Rhodes told officers of her arranged meeting with Babs for 12.30 p.m. the following day at Bradford Interchange student centre; they suggested that she keep it. Gabrielle turned up at the appointed time and waited until almost 1 a.m. before going on to another pub they had visited the previous Friday: the Shoulder of Mutton. There was no Barbara.

In fact, once it was past 12.30 I knew she wasn't going to come. I knew something was gravely wrong. At the back of my mind was the thought of the Ripper. I couldn't get Barbara out of my mind that afternoon and couldn't concentrate. I went back to Barbara's flat and let myself in. There was no one in but J.C.

As police inquiries intensified, the Ripper was preoccupying the minds of senior officers too, particularly that of Detective Chief Superintendent Peter Gilrain, head of West Yorkshire police's western area CID, under whose jurisdiction Bradford fell. If there could be said to be a 'good' time for the infamous killer to strike, this, from the police point of view, was not it.

Assistant Chief Constable in charge of crime George Oldfield had suffered a heart attack, and had been told by doctors to take a complete rest for at least two months before resuming any kind of responsibility. Indeed he had been warned that he stood in grave danger of killing himself if he worked on the case before he was fully recovered. In his place Detective Chief Superintendent Jim Hobson had been appointed acting ACC Crime, but the previous week Mr Hobson had suffered a great personal blow, when his wife fell downstairs at home and fractured her skull. She was in a critical condition and Mr Hobson had been spending as much time as possible at her hospital bedside in Leeds. To make matters worse, Detective Superintendent Dick Holland, indefatigable head of the Ripper Squad itself, had gone to Scotland in a hired motor caravan the previous Friday to begin a fortnight's fishing holiday in the wilds – his first break from the job, apart from occasional Saturday rugby games, since January 1978.

When the telephone rang in the Leach family home on Sunday, David and Beryl Leach were watching the 'Onedin Line' on television.

When I answered the phone a voice asked if Barbara was here. I said, 'No, she comes home on Monday.' I was just going to say I would take a message for her when the policeman told me she had gone for a late night walk and had not returned. It wasn't like her to do this and we immediately thought the worst.

Mr and Mrs Leach were fully aware of the stories about the Yorkshire Ripper that had been appearing in the newspapers, and there followed twenty-six hours of agonized waiting. In fear and dread they sat by the telephone desperate for news. It came. On Monday night at 9.15 p.m. the doorbell rang and a police sergeant and a policewoman told them that Barbara was dead. A body, believed to be that of Barbara, had been found in an alleyway off Back Ash Grove, bundled against a dustbin and covered with a piece of carpeting. A searching police constable had found her at 3.55 p.m. that afternoon, five minutes' walk away from the modern Bradford police headquarters in the Tyrells.

Immediately the body was found the usual police routine got under way. Detective Chief Superintendent Jack Ridgeway of Manchester CID was telephoned and drove to Bradford within an hour of the discovery. Jim Hobson was contacted at Chapel Allerton Hospital, where his wife had just undergone a brain scan and was said to be 'satisfactory'. He and pathologist Professor David Gee rushed to the scene of the crime.

Barbara was fully clothed, her army-type shoulder bag lying nearby. After a preliminary investigation, Professor Gee had her moved to Bradford mortuary to begin his post-mortem, which was to keep him busy until the early hours of Tuesday morning. From an initial examination there was little doubt in his mind that his old adversary the Ripper was responsible – for her massive head wounds, which had covered her body in blood, were all too familiar.

That day Mr and Mrs Leach had to undergo a further ordeal. They were asked to identify Barbara's body in the mortuary in Bradford. They were driven from Kettering to Bradford in a police car which covered the 143 miles in two and a half hours at speeds of over 80 mph. After the identification the police asked them dozens of questions about Barbara's home life, background and social activities, slowly building up a picture of her personality. Later Mr and Mrs Leach met Barbara's student friends, grey-faced and trembling at the tragedy that had struck them all.

Apart from her friends, everyone who lived in the area was being questioned. The backyard in which she was found was rank with grass and weeds, and under the direction of forensic scientists, police officers armed with scythes began to cut swathes through the scrubby growth, to be taken away and minutely examined – an innovation to the

Ripper hunt. When the grass was cut a further team of officers began a hands and knees search.

One of the many students shattered by the news was John McGoldrick of Glasgow, a 22-year-old chemical engineering student who was in his fourth year at Bradford University. He had been at a party at 16 Ash Grove, directly opposite number thirteen, in whose back garden Barbara was found.

There was plenty of noise right into the early hours of Sunday and the window downstairs was wide open. In fact one bloke was lying under the window as I sat talking and drinking with him. We were in full view of the street but saw nothing unusual. It seems incredible that Barbara should have been murdered just a few yards away, while we were drinking so nearby. There is nothing particularly unusual for a girl student to wander around on her own at night in this area; we're a tight-knit community and there is usually someone around.

Barbara had discussed the Yorkshire Ripper with her brother Graham and with friends and had assured everyone that she would not walk unaccompanied after dark in Bradford. Although she liked to go for solitary walks at home in Kettering 'to clear my head for studying', she explained, she was fully conscious of the dangers in the town where the Ripper had killed twice.

Alison Hillman, her former flatmate, began her own campaign in a bid to help police by talking to everyone at the university, urging them to think of any detail which they might have noticed and to take it to the police. Gabrielle Rhodes, too, appealed to her friends and colleagues 'not to forget Barbara'. But the response was disappointing. Officers manning a police mobile unit set up at the corner of Ash Grove reported no more than a couple of callers a day: 'And even they usually only come to ask what we are doing about it, or out of curiosity,' said one.

At a press conference on Wednesday, two days after the body's discovery, Mr Gilrain echoed the complaint. 'I appreciate that it was after 1 a.m. on Sunday when Barbara was attacked,' he said, 'but someone must have seen the killer. Disco dancers, late-night diners, folk going home by taxi in the area, might all be able to help. The public can phone Bradford police, 23422, or use the Ripper Freephone.' He added that it was possible that the killer had been lurking in the streets waiting for people to leave the pub, or had entered the pub earlier and selected his victim.

Meanwhile, in Glenrothis, Scotland, Dick Holland had parked his motor caravan and was having a drink when he heard the news of the murder on television. His four fishing rods still lay in their unopened cases, but all thought of sport and rest left his mind. He turned the caravan around and headed back for West Yorkshire, arriving in time to be briefed by Mr Gilrain before the press conference. He scorned the suggestion that his return had been in any way self-sacrificing.

'I have done nothing else apart from work on this case since January 1978 and was involved in inquiries even before then,' he said. 'I was looking forward to the fortnight's holiday, but having it cut short is just part of a policeman's life. Hopefully I shall have time to take the holiday later.'

Back in Bradford, Dick Holland's first task was to arrange for a reconstruction of Barbara Leach's last walk from the Mannville Arms to the place of her death. Woman Police Constable Barbara Terry, a 24 year old whose build and general appearance matched those of Barbara Leach, volunteered to take the six-minute stroll wearing identical clothing. Peter Gilrain and Dick Holland stayed a few feet behind her, with other officers flanking the road on both sides: for they had a bizarre theory that the Ripper might try and watch the well-publicized reconstruction.

They had said nothing to WPC Terry about the idea, but she sensed it in an eerie fashion.

'I was scared,' she said, 'it was very weird. When I was asked to do the reconstruction I accepted without thinking. When it came to wearing the clothes and actually doing the walk I began to feel a little nervous. I had a funny feeling that the Ripper may be lurking in the background, watching me. I know the way women are reacting to these murders. There is a real fear hanging over almost everyone.'

To supplement the reconstruction, a poster was issued by the police showing WPC Terry with Barbara Leach's head superimposed, hundreds were issued throughout the city. A special appeal was also made in Hindi and Gujerati to Bradford's Asian community by WPC Jagjit Dahele, aged 26, a Kenyan Asian who came to Britain with her family eleven years ago and had been in the force for seven years. Her appeal, broadcast on local radio stations, asked for help 'in catching this monster'.

Sickeningly, there were numerous hoax phone calls and letters to the police within hours of the announcement of the murder; the usual sad reflection on certain sections of the public. Even as WPC Terry completed her walk, for instance, Wakefield police received a phone message from a man claiming to be the Ripper: 'I am going to do another one this weekend,' he said before hanging up. Despite the fact that it was almost certainly a fake call, police were put on full alert throughout the county. Again, a letter sent to a Sheffield newspaper claiming that the next victim would be in Sheffield – several miles south of the usual Ripper territory – was denounced as phoney. The fact remained that all these red herrings took up police time, and the police were in no mood to be trifled with by now.

There were several reasons for their exasperation, but they largely concerned the national press. A number of Fleet Street newspapers, for example, had published old photofit pictures issued by the police years before in an effort to trace witnesses – not the Ripper himself. These had long since been withdrawn by the police and local newspapers were aware of the fact; but it seemed that the nationals had either ignored the withdrawal notice, or had overlooked it.

Most galling of all, however, was the suggestion that Scotland Yard not only should be called in, but *had* been called in. This rumour was the result of a fairly straightforward misunderstanding. At a top-level police conference chaired by the West Yorkshire chief constable, Mr Ronald Gregory, on Friday, 7 September, several senior officers from the north of England police forces had discussed tactics. At the meeting was Mr John Locke, national coordinator for the Regional Crime Squad system – who also happens to be a Scotland Yard deputy assistant commissioner. As most responsible crime reporters well knew, his latter position had nothing to do with his function at the conference, but others implied that Mr Locke had been called in at the express wish of the Home Secretary, William Whitelaw.

The implication was met with cold fury by senior northern officers and dismissed in what were described as 'contemptuous terms' by Mr Gregory. The feeling among detectives at Millgarth police station, Leeds, home of the Ripper incident room, was that any such move might result in the immediate resignation of at least half a dozen of the top officers of superintendent rank and over, including, perhaps, that of Mr Gregory himself. Morale among the Ripper Squad and Area Task Forces would slump from its high pinnacle, and the continuity of the biggest murder investigation that Britain had ever known would be seriously impaired.

Mr Gregory pointed out that, in police circles generally, there had never been any criticism of the way West Yorkshire had handled the difficult and complex investigation. Chief constables and other senior policemen from all over the country had been invited to submit their ideas freely and many had done so. But he also pointed proudly to his force's success in crime fighting. Only two days after Barbara Leach's body was discovered, he had reported to the County Police Committee that crime had fallen by 9½ per cent in the first six months of 1979, and although murder and manslaughter had leapt by 50 per cent with 18 killings compared with 12 in the first half of 1978, 15 of the killers had been detected successfully. One of the unsolved crimes involved the death of Josephine Whitaker in April – the Ripper's eleventh victim. Mr Gregory told Roger Cross, crime correspondent of the *Yorkshire Post*:

I am affronted, and concerned about morale, by talk of Scotland Yard being called in. At no time has there been any question of the men's morale being low and I am confident that the men involved can bring success. If I thought that there was any man elsewhere in the country who could help this inquiry then I would not hesitate to bring him in. But I have never considered asking for help from Scotland Yard, and neither they nor the Home Office have suggested we need their help. It is out of the question.

Despite the ruffled tempers, however, behind the scenes work was going smoothly as the Barbara Leach inquiry entered its second week. An eight-force conference of northern police chiefs was chaired by Mr Gregory at Bradford police headquarters, and though his subsequent press announcement was restricted to such catch-all clichés as 'fruitful' and 'meaningful' the results in the Sunderland area became immediately apparent. Detective Chief Superintendent Ken Barritt, head of the North East Regional Crime Squad, announced that he was putting 50 Sunderland detectives full time on the Ripper case; this brought the manpower in the Ripper's putative home territory to 150, while 300 Yorkshire police officers continued their work at the scene of the latest crime.

On the forensic science front, too, things were moving

apace. A meeting held at the north eastern laboratory at Wetherby, which had handled the forensic side of the Ripper's activities since he began, was called by the Home Office science coordinator, Dr Allan Curry, who later announced that two full-time specialists were to review all scientific evidence gleaned so far.

Perhaps most hopeful, if rather mysterious, was the police pronouncement that they had a 'master plan'. It had, said a spokesman, been evolved after the Whitaker killing in April, and 'reviewed' at the time of the tape being received. No details could be revealed, but they were 'confident' that it would lead to the murderer this time. At the same time, old angles of approach were being reviewed. One involved the Ripper's mention, on the tape, of the time he was disturbed by a uniformed constable in Chapeltown, just before he intended to strike. The woman got away, but, said Mr Hobson, 'she was nearer to death than she realizes'. Despite repeated appeals in the Leeds area she had never been traced, perhaps because she was frightened; he assured her that any information given would be treated in strict confidence and her identity would not be revealed.

There was another possibility, however: the police felt that she might not have heard the tape. It sounded incredible, said Mr Hobson, but he was convinced that many people in the West Riding may neither have heard the tape – available on Freephone – nor seen the published examples of the Ripper's handwriting. Accordingly a massive tour of pubs and clubs – similar to one carried out in Wearside several months previously – was to be carried out. Community inspectors from the fourteen West York-shire divisions would accompany a 'local bobby who knew his patch', playing the tape and showing handwriting samples in an attempt to achieve 'saturation coverage'.

And so the hunt for the Ripper went on, while colleagues at Bradford University planned a lasting memorial to

Barbara Leach, victim number twelve. An official of the university union said that nothing could compensate for the loss of Barbara, but that the executive had agreed, with Barbara's parents' consent, that they would like to introduce some permanent tribute to her contribution to the life of the university.

Graham Leach, Barbara's brother, had been at Cambridge during the period between 1974 and 1976 when the Cambridge rapist hit the headlines. This was a man who wore a black mask with the word RAPIST written across the forehead and who terrorized women in the university town. The reason he later gave to police for his activities was that he had caught syphilis and wanted to pass it on to 'get his own back' on women. Graham said that he and Barbara had discussed crime at that time, and also capital punishment.

She was absolutely against it. So are all the family. The police say they know a lot about this man and when they catch him they will soon be able to prove it is him. We have had dozens of letters from students we don't even know, expressing their sympathy for Barbara's death. My parents are heartbroken. Everyone loved Barbara very much.

On 20 September, 1979 the inquest on Barbara Leach was opened and adjourned by the Bradford coroner, Mr James Turnbull, who then handed a letter to Barbara's father which had been sent to the coroner's office expressing sympathy on behalf of the people of Bradford for the murder.

Two weeks after her death, a campaign to draw the attention of northern people to every aspect of the Ripper's activities was launched; normally, it would have cost almost £1,000,000 but in this case everyone involved – printers, designers, site proprietors, photographers and distributors – gave their services free of charge. The campaign was directed by 37-year-old Graham Poulter, a Leeds advertising executive whose company Graham Poulter Associates,

167

with offices in Leeds, Manchester and London, has an annual turnover of £20,000,000. Fifty of his best people worked on the 'anti-Ripper' drive, at a cost to the company of £120,000. They designed posters ranging from full-sized billboards to flyposters – displayed on over six hundred prime-site billboards throughout the country, especially in the north.

Police also flyposted a total of 5,500 of their own handouts on high-street and other public hoardings. Alongside the police worked the national and daily provincial newspapers, all of whom gave their services freely, either donating advertising space or making up the equivalent in news coverage; newspapers in Northern Ireland concentrated on one theory – thought unlikely but possible – that the Ripper is a soldier who has served tours of duties in the troubled province. BBC local radio stations and independent radio ran tapes of the Ripper, along with police messages – up to eight times a day in the 'target' areas of Yorkshire, Lancashire and the North East. The *Yorkshire Post*, in a leader appealing for public vigilance and the utmost cooperation with the police, said: 'The sickening slaughter of Barbara Leach in Bradford shows the need for almost constant reminders, through the media, that the Yorkshire Ripper will kill and kill and kill, in his own particularly horrible and perverted manner, until caught.'

chapter thirteen

What is the sum total of the damage and the agony caused by the sadistic killer who takes pride in the horrific name, Jack the Ripper? Police headquarters at Wakefield, Yorkshire, will eagerly list the statistics computerized at various stages of the police hunt for the murderer, and the latest, given in August 1979 were: 169,538 people interviewed and eliminated from the inquiry; 161,500 vehicles checked; 23,052 house-to-house searches; 20,245 statements taken; 51,921 lines of inquiry followed; 257 detectives still working full time on the Ripper hunt; more than 3 million pounds spent during the 4 years or so since he first struck in the north of England. The figures become meaningless in the face of the enormity of the police task in tracking him down.

There are other statistics: in the county of Yorkshire the following numbers of children are now motherless as a result of the killings: the 4 children of Wilma McCann; the 3 children of Emily Jackson; the 2 daughters of Irene Richardson, who are with foster parents; the 2 children of Yvonne Pearson; the 3 daughters of Patricia Atkinson. In Lancashire: the 2 children of Jean Royle; the 5 children of Vera Millward, now leading separate lives after the death of their father, and her 2 other children taken to Jamaica by Cy Burkett; the 2 children of Joan Harrison, now with foster parents. In all, 25 children have been made motherless by the Ripper.

That is not all. Behind him he has left a trail of fear and broken lives unequalled in the annals of crime in England. The final effects will never be known, especially on the lives of the children involved. Three women talked of their efforts to rebuild their lives after the Ripper had struck and of the horror that lives with them, and will continue to live with them, for many years to come.

Mrs Maureen Long, one of the four surviving victims, was awarded a further £1,250 interim payment by the Criminal Injuries Compensation Board in August 1979, having refused an outright settlement of £1,500, but taken a £350 interim payment. Her case will be kept under medical review. Mrs Long, mother of three children, said the original offer was 'nothing but an insult, but thanks to my solicitors I am getting more. I don't know what the final amount will be. This money is to keep me going for the next year or so while I have further medical tests. I still have horrific dreams about this madman. I have to take tablets every day. I am still frightened and never move anywhere without someone with me.'

Mrs Olive Smelt, the mother of three children, who was attacked in August 1975, said her life had been ruined by the Ripper. Her husband says that her personality has changed completely. 'The mental scars are still there, and will always be,' he said. 'I remember my wife as full of energy and enjoying a night out with her friends. Now she rarely goes out.' She said: 'At 10 p.m. I am ready for bed and even when I go out, like on New Year's Eve, I am waiting for midnight and ready to go home. I have no interest in anything any more. Nobody deserves anything like that.' Mrs Smelt's young son Stephen, now 13, is most afraid for her. When she is in on her own he makes sure all the doors are locked. She still has her evening cleaning job and he wants her to go to work earlier as winter approaches, so that she can be home before dark. Of the Ripper she says: 'He is a coward. Something must have happened in his life to put him off women, but things happen to a lot of men and they never do anything like this. He has ruined my life.'

Jayne MacDonald's mother expressed strong feelings about the ruination of her family's life together since the murder. She said:

I know exactly how Josephine Whitaker's family must feel. I pray for them. And I pray this killer will be caught. I just keep hoping and praying that if there is a God this monster will be caught and will be stopped from doing these terrible things. I hate the Ripper, whoever he is, for what he did to Jayne and to our family. He has wrecked our family in one way or another. The way I feel I would find some way of killing him myself if he is caught. It seems he believes that any woman out on the street after 11 p.m. is no good. The public obviously disassociated themselves. How many more must die before people wake up and realize it could happen to someone they love. I can understand men who have been prowling in such areas being afraid of admitting it and being afraid of coming forward with information, out of shame or fear. But many of them must be fathers, too, with daughters just like Jayne. I beg them to examine their consciences and ask how they would feel if it happened to their own daughter or wife. The same applies to the killer's own family.

Since the tragedy that struck the MacDonald family, Jayne's youngest sister, Debra, aged 17, has been moody and rebellious, drifting into bad company and telling her mother bitterly: 'It doesn't pay to be good in this world.' She always carries scissors in her handbag for protection. Jayne's brother Ian, aged 14, has become isolated and introvert. He refuses to believe his sister is dead. Janet, now aged 21, after recovering from a near nervous breakdown, found happiness when she married Jayne's ex-boyfriend, who had become one of the family after the death.

Mrs Irene MacDonald, whom neighbours said always entertained them with her jokes and mimicry, finds it impossible to have fun any more. 'You feel so guilty if you smile,' she said. 'Or even if you act naturally and spontaneously. It's the little reminders that crucify you. Like last week when I accidentally knocked over Jayne's musical box and her favourite tune "Raindrops keep falling . . ." tinkled out. It almost destroyed me.' Perhaps most tragic of all for Mrs MacDonald was the fact that her husband, whose hair had turned grey soon after the Ripper's attack on Jayne, suffered a heart attack and died in the late summer of 1979.

chapter fourteen

In the late summer of 1888, five prostitutes in the East End of London were killed by the hand of one man, who described himself in boastful letters to the police as 'Jack the Ripper'. In the 90 years which have elapsed since then, the grisly sobriquet has taken on a significance in criminal history and popular folklore which is out of all proportion to the original murders, and which has been steadily inflated over the years by books, plays, films and television, as well as learned and earnest criminological studies.

Why all the fascination with one deranged knifeman and his five pathetic victims? To begin with, the Victorians – chronic addicts of bloody melodrama – had long been fascinated by the legend of Spring Heeled Jack, who made his appearance in folklore around 1840. Spring Heeled Jack was supposed to be a rapist who bounded towards his victims with unnaturally long, slow strides, his eyes glowing in the dark like coals and his hands those of a beast rather than a man. There were only two vaguely authentic-sounding references to him in the newspapers of the time and even in those no names were given. He was supposed to have raped one girl on Barnes Common, a lonely stretch of open land in west London, and another in Wandsworth, a southern suburb. But very quickly he became superhuman, appearing in children's stories as a sort of avenging demon, in the later versions carrying a huge curved knife.

Very likely memories of this bogeyman – for it is certain that he had no real existence – sprang quickly to the public mind when, on the night of 31 August, a prostitute named Mary Ann Nicholls (or Nichols) was struck down. When her body was found early the following morning police and mortuary attendants were shocked to find that not only had her throat been cut from ear to ear but that her body had been ripped up, twice, from abdomen to breastbone.

Eight days later, the knife attacker claimed his second victim, a consumptive 47-year-old named 'Dark Annie' Chapman. Like the more ebullient Mary Ann Nicholls, Annie Chapman had been turned out of her doss house for want of the few pence charged for a bed, and was wandering the streets looking for a client. Her wounds were even more horrific; the head had been almost severed from the body, and a handkerchief wrapped around it as if to hold it on; the entrails had been pulled out and laid over the shoulder, and the womb and parts of the vagina removed. They were never found.

An enormous hue and cry went up; some members of the public felt the newly immigrant Jews from Eastern Europe were responsible, and there were ugly anti-semitic incidents. The London *Star* suggested that public vigilante committees be set up to stalk the 'unfortunates' who were the killer's potential prey, and that the girls should be 'cautioned to walk in couples'. Some policemen, because of the lack of policewomen in those days, dressed up in women's clothes to walk the streets in the hope of being accosted. Daniel Farson in his book *Jack the Ripper* recounts how this practice led to a hilarious incident in the midst of the horror, when an ambitious journalist decided to dress 'in drag' too. He was stopped by a similarly disguised policeman, who asked him: 'You're a man, aren't you?

Are you one of us?' 'I don't know what you mean,' replied the young journalist indignantly. 'But I'm not a copper if that's what you're referring to.'

Despite massive police saturation of the Whitechapel area – the focus of the first two murders – two more women died on the night of 30 September, within minutes of each other. The first was discovered by a hawker who drove into a yard in his pony and trap and came across the body of Elizabeth Stride. Blood was still pumping from the terrible wounds in her throat, but this time there were no mutilations. The killer had been disturbed. This was at 1 a.m.; three-quarters of an hour later, a policeman in Mitre Square, nearby, found the body of Catherine Eddowes. Eddowes had been slashed about the head, her throat cut and her intestines torn out and flung over her right shoulder – as in the case of Chapman. In Eddowes' case, however, there was a sinister refinement – the left kidney had been removed. Pathologists examining the remaining kidney discovered it to be gin-soaked, and showing traces of Bright's disease. A few days after the double murder, the chairman of the Whitechapel vigilance committee, George Lusk, received a gruesome parcel. It contained half a human kidney, later established to be identical with that remaining in Eddowes' body. With it was a letter, addressed: 'From Hell.' It said:

'Mr Lusk Sir I send you half the Kidne I took from one woman prasarved it for you, tother piece I fried and ate it was very nice . . .' (sic)

Previously, he had sent a letter to the chief of the Central News Agency, signing himself 'Jack the Ripper' and warning of the double killings.

The Ripper's final victim was Mary Kelly, or Marie Jeanette Kelly, as she liked to call herself. Unlike her predecessors under the knife she was relatively pretty and only twenty-five; she seems to have done sufficiently well on the streets to be able to rent a small room for herself for four shillings a week. It was here, on the night of 8 November, that she died. With each killing the Ripper had become more ferocious, and Mary Kelly's death was probably a literal bloodbath. At least one Ripper expert believes that her killer must have stripped and put his clothes well out of the way before attacking her while they were both naked. Blood soaked the bed through and was spattered everywhere in the room from the ceiling to the far corners of the floor.

Because he was indoors the Ripper was able to take his time with Mary Kelly. She was literally hacked to pieces. Her nose, ears and lips had been cut away, her breasts removed and placed on a bedside table, her entrails hung around the walls of the room, her rib cage entirely exposed and her thighs carved to the bone like hams.

The landlord, who saw the body, recalled later: 'I had heard a great deal about the Whitechapel murders, but I declare to God I had never expected to see such a sight as this.'

After the death of Kelly, Jack the Ripper faded away into the mists of Whitechapel and of history. There were no further murders, and although many claimed to be him – including Dr Neil Cream, who poisoned a number of prostitutes some years later, and 'confessed' on the gallows – it is almost certain that he committed suicide.

Even as the murders were taking place, the legends were growing, fed in part by the ambience of the era and the time of year. London's East End in those days was still a warren of narrow streets, marked out for the most part in late medieval times; they were ill-lit, and the autumn mists from the nearby Thames combined with the thick smoke from hundreds of chimneys to produce a sulphurous yellow smog. It muffled noises, reduced the figures of pedestrians to shapeless silhouettes, and laid pale haloes around the few street gas lamps.

As Sir Melville Macnaughten, head of Scotland Yard's

CID at the time, wrote many years later: 'No one who was living in London will forget the terror caused by those murders. Even now I remember the foggy evenings and the cries of the newspaper boys, "Another 'orrible murder, murder, mutilation, Whitechapel."' One woman, Mrs Mary Burridge, was so distressed when she read of the details of Annie Chapman's death that she had a fit and died, still clutching the newspaper.

All this was sensational material for newspapers, and later for novelists and horror film producers. But the real, continuing interest to criminolgoists is the random nature of the crimes. What were the Ripper's motives? For years he was popularly supposed to be either a slaughterman or a surgeon who had, perhaps, been infected by a prostitute, or had decided to wage a holy war against them. In no case had the Ripper attempted to have sexual intercourse with the girls; in the first four cases at least, evidence showed that he had slashed their throats from behind and then ripped them up with a long sharp knife. After studying old photographs and drawings discovered in the early 1970s, the late Professor Francis Camps, Home Office pathologist, dismissed the medical man theory as absurd. 'Any surgeon who operated in this manner,' he said, 'would have been struck off the medical register.'

The Ripper himself, in letters to the police and the press, gave two reasons for what he was doing; firstly, he hated prostitutes, and secondly, he seemed to take pleasure in the cat and mouse game he was playing with the police. In his letter to the Central News Agency he said, in part:

'*Dear Boss, I keep on hearing that the police have caught me but they won't fix me just yet. I have laughed when they look so clever and talk about being on the right track . . . I am down on whores and shan't quit ripping them until I do get buckled . . .*'

But there was obviously more to the killer's course of action than that; the French called him 'Jacques L'Evrentreur'

– Jack the Stomach-opener – and Colin Wilson, in his *Casebook of Murder*, echoes the phrase in a theory which won the approval of Francis Camps and many forensic psychiatrists:

The Ripper was not interested in genitals; his fantasies were all about cutting bellies. It was the womb itself that fascinated him. Freudians will draw a great many inferences from this – about hatred of the mother, perhaps of younger brothers and sisters stealing the parent's affection, etc. I would draw only one inference: that this destruction of the womb indicated a suicidal tendency in the Ripper; it was the place that bore him about which he felt ambivalent.

There are many other examples of 'motiveless murders' in criminal history; some of a sexual nature and others, such as the unsolved 'zodiac' murders on America's west coast, of no apparent nature at all. The general feeling among psychiatrists is that a man impelled to kill at random, like a man impelled to expose himself, say, first fantasizes about committing the act, and then tries it out. He is satisfied for a while, and then does it again, and again, becoming more reckless each time. He almost certainly feels a period of guilt for what he has done, but is able to push that guilt out of his mind. But after a while the need to commit another act surges to the fore again. Eventually the clash between the urge and the remorse it produced may become so great that he might either give himself up, become so careless that he is caught or, in extreme cases, commit suicide.

This may be the case with the Yorkshire Ripper; almost certainly it was so in the case of his predecessor. There have been various theories about the identity of the East End ripper: that he was the Duke of Clarence, grandson of Queen Victoria; the painter Walter Sickert; Peduchenko, a Russian surgeon who was also an anarchist; Sir William Gull, the Queen's surgeon, and so on. The most likely candidate is the one favoured by Daniel Farson in his book *Jack the Ripper*, written after Mr Farson gained access to the private papers of Sir Melville Macnaughten. Macnaughten's chief suspect was a quiet, unassuming lawyer named Montagu John Druitt whose practice, in the East End, was a failure, whose mother had gone mad, and who feared that he too was going out of his mind. Druitt drowned himself in the Thames shortly after the last killing.

There is an uncanny similarity between the phrases used by the old Ripper and the new Ripper, and to compare them, we chose random sentences from the original Ripper's letter, sent to the editor of the Central News Agency, London, in 1888, and other sentences from the letters and tape sent to George Oldfield. Here's how they compare:

1888	1979
Dear Boss	Dear Officer
I keep on hearing the police have caught me	I see you are still having no luck catching me
But they won't fix me just yet	You are no nearer catching me now than four years ago when I started
I have laughed when they looked so clever and talked about being on the right track	The only time they came near catching me was a few months back in Chapeltown when I was disturbed
I am down on whores	There's plenty of them knocking about. They never learn, do they, George?
I shan't quit ripping them until I do get buckled	I'll keep on going for quite a while yet
I love my work and want to start again	I'm not quite sure when I will strike again
How can they catch me now?	I can't see myself being nicked just yet
You will soon hear of me and my funny little games	Hope you like the catchy tune at the end, ha ha
Yours Truly, Jack the Ripper	Yours, Jack the Ripper

chapter fifteen

Jack the Ripper is alive in England today and he has proved that he will kill any woman who walks alone after dark. Over two thousand people have told the police they suspect they know him. It is clear that someone – mother, wife, grandparents – knows him and is protecting him. It is also possible that he has a brother or sister or close workmate who has strong suspicions but will not speak out because of a false sense of loyalty. The original Jack the Ripper escaped because methods of criminal detection were in their infancy in the 1880s. The Yorkshire Ripper has matched his cunning against the most modern methods of crime detection, confidently believing that he leaves no clues, that there are no fingerprints and that all is 'as clean as a whistle', in his own phrase. When he is caught, or is found dead, having committed suicide in despair once the pressure of containing his secret about the ghastly murders becomes too much for him to bear, it will be revealed just how much evidence the police have against him. But there is always a nagging doubt in the mind of the senior police officer in charge: 'How much should I make public? If I reveal some of the clues, will it help the Ripper to destroy what would later be evidence admissible in a court of law? Or will the publicity catch the eye of that one person who says: "I know him." If I issue a photograph of the type of workbench tools he uses to hack and mutilate his victims, and his boot size and rare blood group etc., will it help to flush him out or give him a chance to destroy evidence?'

It is an agonizing decision for one man to make.

In order to hunt him down the police themselves must surmise what kind of man the Ripper is. Each time he grappled with one of the victims, he must have left some trace of himself behind: a hair from his head, from his forearm, a piece of skin, a tiny drop of blood, a smear of oil, a metal chip or filing. They know the type of industrial boot he wears and his boot size (small in the range of men's boot sizes) and practically everything about the car he uses. This evidence will be used against the man if he comes to trial. But what about the other side of the Ripper, his mentality and his behaviour pattern?

Dr Stephen Shaw, consultant psychiatrist at Stanley Royds Hospital, Wakefield, spoke of his theory:

The Ripper is an over-controlled aggressive psychopath, who can function in society but as stress mounts and mounts there is a catharsis. He is likely to be a young man, highly intelligent, but he could score very low on any normal intelligence scales. He has a degree of innate native cunning, an aggressive psychopath with a paranoid streak who has invested prostitutes with a real or imaginary wrong, and is waging a crusade – a holy war – against them.

The stresses and strains of individuals are *individual*. Subtle changes occur in his behaviour which only a wife or a workmate would notice. There has been a gap of fifty-four weeks between two of the murders. This could be a quiescent phase. He might have been a soldier in Northern Ireland, on holiday, or abroad. He will feel no remorse after committing a murder. He undoubtedly reads about himself in the newspapers, but I doubt if he keeps a scrapbook. I think he is clever enough not to. I doubt if he has a violent background, although later his family may look back on certain little incidents and say, 'Ah, yes, such and such happened years ago.' He does not panic. He must be covered in blood but he goes home carefully, calm as anything. He wouldn't drive fast through the streets and invite the police to stop him. He is not copying the first Jack the Ripper, except in name. That Ripper murdered six women in a period of six weeks. This one is in a different league altogether.

There is a remote chance he may have confided in someone – dropped hints. He is certainly a perfectionist. He will be caught by sheer dogged detective work, or he may just disappear, and that will be the end of it.

After the murder of Josephine Whitaker, Dr Rod Watson, senior lecturer in sociology at Manchester University, whose special subject is the interrogation of murder suspects, talked at length about the mind of the Ripper, saying:

It is not beyond the bounds of possibility that he saw this girl walking home across the park and decided that since she was alone and it was so late that she was acting like a prostitute and was, in fact, inviting the crime. This is how he would justify it to himself. Or it could be that he is focusing on some trait which he dislikes in prostitutes and which he now sees echoed in other women. It could be anything – from the way they walk to the kind of clothes they wear. We have to remember that this chap is mentally ill and mental illness is not a static thing; it is dynamic and it shifts and changes. I feel pretty certain he has a thing about loose morality and that this is still the motive behind the killings.

Dr Watson said he was particularly disturbed by the Whitaker murder because the Ripper made a radical change in the area he chose for the killing – an open area in a respectable neighbourhood.

At any moment, either in the act of murder or coming away from it, he could have been seen by someone walking a dog or driving a car across the park. This suggests to me that he is becoming bolder and taking greater risks. Before he took just enough of a risk to make sure his victims would be found. Now I think he is taking the kind of risks which I believe will eventually lead to him being caught in the act. When you think of the houses around the park, the roads, the people in cars, you have to be pretty cool to take the risk that absolutely no one is going to see you.

Dr Watson said he agreed with the police view that the Ripper enjoys his notoriety. 'This kind of murderer also enjoys the fear he causes among the population at large. It is a form of terrorism.' He thought it wrong to produce a psychological identi-kit picture of the Ripper:

If you are working on a definite profile, you don't bother to look elsewhere and this type of murder cuts right across the social spectrum. He could be a labourer or a white collar worker. He could live alone or with his mother, or he could be a married man with a family. It is possible that he could have a record of mental illness but I would judge, on the basis of the evidence so far, that he could prove to be someone with only a minor history of mental illness or even no record at all. In any case the police will have checked all the records at psychiatric hospitals in West Yorkshire long ago.

Quite often in cases like this, the public tend to get a mental picture of a fiend stalking the streets. In fact, murderers of this kind present an ordinary façade, going about their business and carrying on their social life in an everyday way. What they have done is far from normal but they look normal and that is what makes them so difficult to catch.

Dr Watson pointed out that the Boston Strangler was an ordinary plumber, married with a family, and that not even his wife knew what he was doing. David Berkowitz, the 'Son of Sam', who murdered six women at the instigation of 'voices' telling him to do it, was a postman, described by his colleagues as 'a nice guy, obedient and gentle'.

He believes the Ripper could come from a community where relationships with the police are bad or possibly non-existent. This being so there would be less chance of anyone giving him away simply because there is no information flow from that community to the police. Such communities, both in this country and in the United States, close ranks. He has said of the difficulties confronting police:

I don't believe people understand what an enormous problem the police have with this type of crime. They come under tremendous pressure, but really, what have they got to go on? This man leaves no definite clues, no murder weapons, no fingerprints, nothing. So the police are left trying to figure out who the hell it might be from several million strangers. With the best forensic experts in the world it is still like trying to find the proverbial needle in the haystack. I would bet he has no previous police record at all, otherwise a three million pound search, which is what this has become, would have come up with something by now.

In the United States there is sufficient evidence to show that certain mentally deranged killers are affected by the moon and this is now taken seriously by the police and charts are studied. It has helped in several cases and I would certainly be looking at this aspect if I were engaged on the Ripper case. I think it is highly likely that this man will be caught in the act, unlike his Victorian counterpart who ceased to kill and was never discovered. The fact that he is now choosing much more public places for the victim is an indication that he may one day become over-confident and make a fatal slip. But I don't think it will happen tomorrow and unfortunately there may be more murders before it does happen. And I still feel he has it in for prostitutes and if there is another victim, it will be a prostitute again.

One of the things which gives these murders their awful continuity is the mutilations found on the bodies (police officers in Yorkshire who were shown slides of the victims were so sickened that some of them had to leave the room) because the killer is not satisfied with merely killing his victims. He has to dehumanize the women he has murdered to the level of objects. Mutilations always represent a massive degradation of the human being. In the United States, when killers like this are caught, one oftens finds that they are religious-minded men who seriously believe they have done the world a service in ridding the community of members of such stigmatized groups as prostitutes, homosexuals, tramps and ethnic minorities. Deviants like the Ripper are people who carry ordinary moral values to an illogical conclusion. They over-dramatize the moral values and translate them into vicious acts of persecution. By stigmatizing people like prostitutes, who then drift into certain areas of our cities, we ourselves make it easier for the deviants to find them.

Murderers like the Ripper, almost without exception, speak of their crimes quite matter of-factly. They present the murder or murders as a very trivial part of their lives.

On the basis of the hard evidence of the letters and the tape recording, what can we now surmise about the Ripper? We must start in the town of Sunderland, within a fifteen-mile radius of which his accent is placed, and also where the letters were posted. The handwriting indicates that he attended an elementary school which gave a good grounding in English grammar, although he may not have been a good student. He knows where to put the apostrophes but not the full stops. The phrasing shows his pedantry: *'about a year'* and then *'to be exact'*, for he is *trying* to be exact. During the 1950s the Marion Richardson style of handwriting was introduced into many Sunderland schools. This is the very rounded form of lettering, almost imitating the type of lettering an infant-school teacher would write on a black-board. This method was a breakaway from the old 'copper-plate' style of handwriting previously taught throughout schools in the north east of England, which could indicate that the Ripper's schooling ended before the 1950s. After the Josephine Whitaker murder, George Oldfield put his age between 30 and 55 – not a very sure assessment, but the mean average would put his age at $42\frac{1}{2}$. If the Ripper was born between 1936 and 1937 and started school at 5 years in 1941 and stayed at school for 10 years, leaving at the age of 15 (the normal school-leaving age at the time on Wearside) in 1951 the slanting 'copperplate' handwriting was still being taught in Sunderland.

Again, assuming that he was 42 in 1979, he would have had to do National Service in the period 1955-7 from the age of 18 to 20. If he was an apprentice engineer, electrical fitter or mechanical fitter he could have been given a deferment, or, as many 18 year olds did at that time, go into the services for two years and 'get it over with'. The armed forces took many of these partly trained men in the engineering industry, and trained them for their own needs during their periods of National Service. A highly qualified engineer with, for example, City and Guilds qualifications, could go into the Royal Navy as an engineering officer. Less qualified 'fitters' could go into the RAF and be trained to service jet engines, or go into the Army as Royal Electrical Mechanical Engineers. An alternative which many young engineers took was to go into the Merchant Navy and thus avoid having to do National Service. Many Geordie engineers preferred the freedom of the MN and its tradition of drinking and world-wide travel to the more rigorous discipline of the Royal Navy, Royal Air Force or the British Army.

On the tape recording, the Ripper uses two expressions which indicate that he left Wearside for a few years. After a period in the south of England or in the services, most Geordies drop their native 'Aa'm' to the more understandable 'I'm', which the Ripper has done. And he uses the expression 'top', meaning 'kill' – a slang expression used only in London in the 50s and 60s, and which spread north after that, when police serials on television allowed the 'villains' to use realistic speech.

The other curiosity about the tape is the Ripper's use of the expression 'Lord', as if there is a strong religious influence in his background or in his thinking. He clearly looks upon himself as some kind of avenging angel, destroying 'scarlet women' who are out alone on the streets after midnight. On the tape he tends to salivate and slur his words slightly, and at the end, when he laughs that dead, hollow laugh, it is totally without mirth or humour.

So what kind of background could this terrifying man have had? His early years would have been deprived, because of the war years and rationing which followed. His home would have been a brick back-to-back, possibly with an outside midden – a privy into which cinders were occasionally poured – and cold water taps. He probably saw his father bathe in a tin bath in front of the coal fire and then had to use the same water to save his mother boiling every pan and kettle in the house to fill it again. When he started work at 15 he would have had to suffer the freezing winters of Wearside, leaving for the factory or shipyard at 6.30 a.m. to start at 7 a.m. in the dark. He may have spent Saturday afternoons at Roker Park, watching a football match, and his hobby was probably tinkering with a bicycle, motor-cycle or, later, an old car, for he appears to be a skilful motorist, maintaining at low cost an old 'banger' over a four-year period.

The police say he is an 'engineer – in the widest sense' and he would probably be flattered to be called an 'engineer'. He does not bother to dress up when he goes out on his Saturday night expeditions in search of a victim – does not even bother to change his work boots or work trousers (probably blue jeans) while driving around the streets. During his teenage years he may have gone to dance halls on Saturday nights 'dressed up' and wearing his best suit, looking for a girl-friend. It is possible he may have been consistently rejected by girls because of a physical defect, or he may have discovered then that he was impotent and has nursed his shame ever since.

The police have speculated on various reasons for his hatred of women: that he may have been rejected by his wife; that he may have caught a venereal disease from a prostitute; that his mother may have been a prostitute; that he was rejected by a prostitute. But as one of the surviving victims, Mrs Olive Smelt, says, lots of men are rejected by women but do not go around killing them because of that. The reason surely lies deep in his childhood. A likely explanation is that he has an aged parent – possibly his mother – living in Sunderland or one of the mining villages around the Wear, and visits her for her birthday in March, when he posts the letters to the police. March is not a normal holiday month, so he has a good reason for returning to his native soil during that month. His mother may be a religious woman who turned him away from 'bad women' as a young boy, or his father may have gone with prostitutes and flaunted the fact before his wife and son, causing a break-up in the marriage, a ruination of the boy's security. He has a burning hatred of prostitutes, referring to them as if they are lower than vermin.

In his tape to George Oldfield he says: '*There's plenty of* them *knocking about.* They *never learn, do* they*, George? I bet you warned* them*, but* they *never listen*' (our emphasis), and the impression is that he doesn't need to say who he means by '*them*' and '*they*' – that he and a senior police officer are respectable citizens, on the *right* side of the law, and the Ripper is only helping society by ridding it of '*them*'. He is partly the groveller: '*Dear Officer*', posing as a law-abiding citizen: '*I have the greatest respect for you, George*', then taunting by implying that Oldfield can't be much good as a policeman, and threatening: '*I warned you in March that I'd strike again.*' He shows his pedantic manner: '*definitely*' some time this year, '*maybe*' September or October. And he keeps his word: he will be on time, he will not let the police down. The deep puritanical streak in his make-up shows itself by his desire to emphasize his dependability.

What kind of person would he be at work? Although he is a loner, he probably wants to be 'one of the boys' in the public house, and wants to join in the laughter when a 'dirty' joke is told. He may at some time have expressed his hatred of prostitutes at work, in a sudden burst of rage, calling them 'dirty bitches' or something similar, then recovering himself in case he shows his hand. He probably pretends his sex life is normal, or jokes about the 'conquests' he has or has had with prostitutes, and may make remarks like: 'If I want a woman I rent one – by the hour' or something to indicate a masculinity which he knows in secret he does not possess. He may buy 'girlie' magazines and stare at the nudes, and later, secretly, tear them up in a rage and destroy them so that his mother, perhaps, does not find them.

Psychiatrists have speculated whether or not he would have a collection of press clippings about himself. One school of thought is that he is too cunning, and the other that, like American psychopaths of his type, he has cuttings, tape, and even video-tape of his exploits, but keeps them hidden in a secret 'hiding-hole' that even intimate family could not find.

George Oldfield has consistently said that he believes the Ripper lives in West Yorkshire, merely posting the letters from the north east to mislead the police. How does the Ripper cope with the fact that when he leaves the scene of the murder he is wearing blood-soaked clothing and foot-wear and carrying blood-stained implements? One theory is that he may have access to a boiler-house or heating appliance where he can either wash and dry clothes quickly, or destroy them in a furnace after each killing. He may even live on or have access to factory premises where no one would notice him entering at, say, 3 a.m. on a Sunday morning and washing clothes and workbench tools under a running cold tap – cold water being the easiest way to soak out blood.

If the police arrest the Ripper, what are they likely to find, apart from forensic evidence? During the summer of 1978 the librarian at Sunderland central library discovered that all the books on the original Jack the Ripper had been stolen from the library. He told the police and detectives questioned the staff. One of the easiest crimes to commit in Britain is stealing books from a public library. A potential thief walks in, takes the books, puts them inside his coat and leaves by a fire exit. No one in England needs to have an identity card, so librarians issue library tickets if the applicant simply gives a name which is on the electoral register, or says he is staying at that address. The library assistant will even fill in the application card if the person applying seems simple or claims to be confused about the right way to apply. It is possible that the person who stole the books from Sunderland library was the Ripper himself, although the staff were unable to help the police, who later told them to treat the matter as confidential.

The only items known to be missing from the scenes of the murders were some jewellery taken from the body of Joan Harrison, and Wilma McCann's purse. The police working on the hunt for the Ripper can expect an arrest from only five directions of pursuit:

1 The slow process of eliminating engineers in firms whose vast numbers fill a book the size of a telephone directory, by comparing handwriting on work-cards, and finding that dates of absence from the engineering works coincide with the dates on which the letters were posted.

2 His car number: if police who are staking out red light areas have the luck that he goes into their net. In the case of Barbara Leach, however, he was in a student bed-sit area, not the Lumb Lane–Manningham red light areas.

3 A straight tip-off from someone who, after reading this book, for example, thinks they know him and makes a telephone call.

4 Being caught in the act. He is trying to make fools of the police, and is taking bigger and bigger chances. A member of the public seeing a man attack a woman may make a call which would trap the Ripper, but would probably not save the woman's life.

5 Birthplace records, or school or apprenticeship records followed up and an old acquaintance's memory being jogged. Britain's most experienced dialect expert, Professor Stanley Ellis, has compared the voices of men in the mining village of Castletown, on the River Wear, to the voice on the Ripper tape, and police have visited the two thousand dwellings there. The methodical search continues to other Wearside mining villages in the hope that someone will recognize the voice.

To sum up: in his room he may have a collection of press clippings about the Yorkshire Ripper; a collection of books on the original Jack the Ripper, whom he 'bettered' by sending a tape-recording of his voice to taunt the police; some jewellery belonging to Joan Harrison, murdered in Preston; or an even more macabre souvenir: a little white plastic purse with MUMIY written on it in biro, by nine-year-old Sonje McCann.

One thing is sure – he is here today, living and working in Britain, leading his double life, revelling in his ghastly secret. He may even be looking over your shoulder, reading these words . . .

IF YOU THINK YOU KNOW HIM, TELEPHONE FREEPHONE 5050

Acknowledgements

This book was written during the summer and early autumn of 1979, in Yorkshire. During the course of its preparation, the authors conducted numerous interviews with policemen, reporters, prostitutes, club owners, barmen, taxi drivers, and the ordinary residents of the Leeds–Bradford–Manchester area. Some individuals, however, helped us particularly with advice and background information and to these we owe a special debt of thanks: to Detective Superintendents Dick Holland and Jack Slater, who gave us a valuable interview at Halifax; the ever generous and affable Inspector Roy Spencer, of Millgarth Police headquarters, Leeds; Sergeant Barry Shaw, editor of the *West Yorkshireman* police newspaper, and Bob Baxter, Graham King and Penny Veal of the West Yorkshire Metropolitan Police press office; chief reporter Derek Hudson and crime correspondent Roger Cross of the *Yorkshire Post*; news editor Peter Hinchliffe and his crime staff Neil Atkinson and Val Javons of the *Huddersfield Daily Examiner*; Denis Walsh of BBC Radio Leeds; Winnie Walsh of the *Manchester Evening News*; Rod Hopkinson of the *Bradford Telegraph and Argus*; and Malcolm Oddy of Hopkinson's news agency for insights into the growth of the immigrant communities in Bradford.

We would like to stress, however, that the persons named are in no way responsible for any mistakes which may have occurred in this account; any errors of judgement or omissions are the authors' alone.

Peter Kinsley
Frank Smyth

Gerold Frank
The Boston Strangler £1.50

The most bizarre series of murders since Jack the Ripper ...
Albert DeSalvo, brutal sexual psychopath who murdered thirteen
women and held a city in the icy grip of terror for eighteen
hideous months.

'Gerold Frank omits nothing about the murders ... or about the
pathetic victims ... he tells us everything about the case and he
tells it chronologically, as it happened ... the result is completely
satisfying' NEW YORKER

Jeffrey Iverson
More Lives than One? 75p

Under Arnall Bloxham's hypnosis more than four hundred
ordinary people have tape-recorded amazingly detailed accounts
of their past lives – accounts so authentic that they can only be
explained by the certainty of reincarnation. A Welsh housewife
describes the massacre of Jews in 12th century York ... A press
photographer remembers watching the execution of Charles I in
Whitehall in 1649 ...

Foreword by Magnus Magnusson.